REBELS AND VICTIMS

Kennikat Press
National University Publications
Literary Criticism Series

General Editor
John E. Becker
Fairleigh Dickinson University

Rebels and Victims

The Fiction of Richard Wright and Bernard Malamud

EVELYN GROSS AVERY

National University Publications
KENNIKAT PRESS / 1979
Port Washington, N.Y. / London

Manufactured in the United States of America

Published by
Kennikat Press Corp.
Port Washington, N.Y. / London

Library of Congress Cataloging in Publication Data

Avery, Evelyn Gross, 1940–
    Rebels and victims.

    (Literary criticism series) (National university publications)
    Bibliography: p.
    Includes index.
    1. American fiction—20th century—History and criticism. 2. Wright, Richard, 1908–1960—Criticism and interpretation. 3. Malamud, Bernard—Criticism and interpretation. 4. Afro-Americans in literature. 5. Jews in literature. I. Title.
PS379.A9   813'.03   79-4362
ISBN 0-8046-9234-3

To my husband and sons

CONTENTS

PREFACE

Twenty years ago when I was an English major at Brooklyn College, ethnic literature was virtually invisible. We studied frontier comedy, but not ghetto humor, colonial diaries, but not slave narratives. Richard Wright and Bernard Malamud were names in library catalogs, but rarely in American literature courses. At the time few seemed to share my interest in ethnic writers.

Fortunately the situation changed. Years later I met Professor Christof Wegelin of the University of Oregon, who encouraged me to undertake this study. A fine scholar and a good friend, Professor Wegelin carefully read the manuscript, offered excellent advice, and continually expressed confidence in my work. I have also benefitted from corresponding and meeting with Bernard Malamud, who has generously responded to my questions and indicated interest in this book. Similarly I am grateful to Professor Jan Wilkotz and Professor Dan Jones, my colleagues at Towson State University, who read the manuscript and provided useful comments. In addition I would like to thank the American Association of University Women whose fellowship enabled me to work on this book.

Finally, I want to acknowledge the contributions of my family. Though uneducated, my grandmother, Jenny Pittelman encouraged me to attend college. Her interest in people and their stories continue to influence my work. My hard-working parents, Fay and Jack Gross also deserve praise for their faith in me. Though their opportunities were limited, they believed that my future would be brighter. Most of all I want to thank my husband Don and my sons, Peter and Daniel for their respect, tolerance, and cooperation. Though quite young, the children limited their demands and tried to satisfy mine. For his part Don deserves much of the credit for this project. Enthusiastic and helpful, he was willing to read, discuss, and made worthwhile comments on my work. More importantly, his encouragement and love have inspired me and make this book possible.

REBELS AND VICTIMS

ABOUT THE AUTHOR

Evelyn Gross Avery has a Ph.D. in American literature with a concentration in ethnic literature from the University of Oregon. Her teaching experience includes two years in East Africa, three years in Oregon colleges, and five years at Towson State University in Baltimore, Maryland, where she is currently Professor of English. She is an active member of MELUS, Society for the Study of Multi-Ethnic Literature of the U.S., having served on its executive board, and currently contributes to its journal. Dr. Avery also edits *Kaleidoscope,* a multi-ethnic newsletter.

Introduction

> The rebel denies without saying No to life, the
> victim succumbs without saying Yes to oppres-
> sion. Both acts are, in a sense, identical: they
> affirm the human against the nonhuman.
>
> Ihab Hassan, *Radical Innocence*

Twentieth-century Western man has been repeatedly analyzed,
defined, and labelled. Poets, philosophers, social scientists, literary
critics, have all dissected this product of a technological age and
concluded similarly: the age of conformity has arrived. A mass,
industrialized society leaves little opportunity for individual heroics.
In a machine age the individual's capacity to determine events is
reduced. Manfred gives way to Babbitt. The Olympian spirit disappears; the "hollow men" proliferate. Gatsby's star is dimmed;
Frederick Henry's life loses purpose. Alienation becomes the key
word. Man seems adrift in a world where differences have disappeared, traditional values have become meaningless. Though sur-
feited with material prosperity, the individual is dissatisfied, feels
impotent; his identity is threatened.

Seeking escape from a mundane existence, he is attracted by the
exotic, the bizarre, the different. The outsider, the man set apart by
race, culture, actions becomes the focus of attention. Interest in the
outsider is particularly evident in the United States with its increasingly mobile, rootless population. American theater, cinema, music,
and literature reflect this absorption. The marginal man, alienated
from American society and values, dominates post–World War Two
novels like *The Victim, Invisible Man,* and *The Naked and the Dead*
to name but a few.

Not surprisingly, many Jewish and Negro protagonists appear in
contemporary fiction. Their experience with persecution makes them

3

experts in alienation, "gifted with a double vision both inside and outside of [American] culture."[1] Their fates reflect the alternatives offered those who reject conformity, who struggle for individual identity.[2] A clear pattern of behavior emerges in Afro-American and Jewish-American fiction. The marginal man, Jew or Negro, confronting a harsh environment, the scorn of fellow citizens, physical and psychological oppression, can either internalize his frustration, suffering inwardly as a victim, or become a rebel, striking out at others. The victim accepts his predicament, elevating pain to a moral virtue; the rebel responds violently in an attempt to survive. While both types have appeared in Jewish and Negro fiction, the tendency in recent ethnic novels has been for the black to assume the archetypal role of rebel, the Jew, the role of victim.[3] The distinction between rebel and victim is not in their suffering (though the nature of that may differ) but in their response to it.

While much of earlier fiction (both black and white) depicted the Negro as simple and satisfied, humble and grateful—a smiling, shuffling innocent—more recent works have rejected this image. Uncle Tom and Sambo have disappeared from contemporary black literature. The black rebel, driven to assert himself, often violently, has replaced the acquiescent victim. Some critics have argued that one stereotype has merely replaced another.[4] But even these analysts recognize that the image of the Negro has changed. The writer most frequently credited with making the Negro "visible" is Richard Wright. Echoing others, Saunders Redding, a noted black author, has stated "that there is . . . no Negro writer now at work, who has not felt the tremendous influence of Dick Wright."[5] "Wright is [recognized] as the father of the contemporary Black writer because when we come to [his] best work we are faced with the central question about being black in America."[6] Offering historical and sociological, as well as psychological insights into the American character, Wright examines the rebel, his behavior and motivations, his background. Products of a lower-class black environment, Wright's rebels are well acquainted with hunger, disease, poverty. They learn quickly from frightened mothers and beaten fathers not to expect much from America. Their dreams of power are undercut by the reality of Jim Crow and more subtle discrimination. Ambition is discouraged; impotency reinforced. All entrances and exits are blocked. Trapped, Wright's black man may choose to suffer his fate passively; he may reluctantly accept his status as a victim. But not for long. Wright's victims are generally minor characters or else they evolve into sullen rebels. Suffering is tolerated, not valued as morally uplifting as it frequently is in Jewish literature.

In sharp contrast to the black rebel, Jewish writers from Sholom Aleichem to Bernard Malamud have depicted Job-like victims who may question their trials but ultimately accept suffering as a possible good. Compared with blacks in contemporary fiction, the Jewish victims of European and American literature generally reject violence and often welcome their burdens. They embrace "a vision in which some subtle purposiveness to history always managed to reassert itself in the face of repeated horror."[7] Despite the objections of Robert Alter, Cynthia Ozick, and a few other critics, critical evidence suggests that Bernard Malamud's writing "represents the most consistent . . . recent attempt to blend the traditional Yiddish folktale with the modern American scene and its values. Malamud most resembles such Yiddish masters as I. L. Peretz, Mocher Seforim, and Sholom Aleichem in his concern for morality and ethics."[8]

Like Wright, who depicts the Southern and Northern, the rural and urban black man, Malamud portrays Jews in a variety of settings, American and European, country and city. But despite the variation of locale, a consistent pattern dominates the lives of rebels and victims. Malamud's Jews, though not as oppressed as Wright's Negroes, are often lower-class, economically marginal. Their homes and shops, which may be rat free, are nonetheless dark, depressing places, often described as "tombs" and "graves." Like Wright's, some of Malamud's victims are products of broken homes, battered families. Still, Malamud's American Jews have possibilities for materially improving their lives. Paradoxically, they usually reject these opportunities, choosing to sacrifice comfort for the spiritual rewards of suffering. They often begin as Wright's characters do, desiring security and status but end by renouncing these objectives, having discovered that love, discipline, responsibility are more important. Confronted with adversity, the rebel, on the other hand, projects his frustration onto others, thus freeing himself. The victim who attempts this finds his freedom reduced, his spirit imprisoned by guilt. Self-contempt, helplessness suffered by both victims and rebels translate into acts of love by the former, hatred by the latter.

The image of Jewish victim and black rebel in contemporary

fiction has been remarkably consistent and appears in the works of both Malamud and Wright.[9]

> The Negro . . . whether thought of as killer or pious slave, has always represented for the American imagination the primitive and the instinctive. . . . The Jew . . . stands symbolically for the uses and abuses . . . of intelligence. They represent the polar opposition of law and lawlessness, the eternal father and the eternal child. . . . [For many] the Negro [is associated with] visceral, impulsive joy in life . . . while the Jew, cerebral, talkative, melancholy is the enemy of his own sexuality.[10]

The "cerebral, talkative," physically timid Jew, agonizing over every act, is a trademark of Malamud's fiction. His lonely characters search for meaning in life, are driven repeatedly to explain themselves and their circumstances. Regardless of class, storekeepers, craftsmen, scholars, artists all "blend into one character: the student of life";[11] an ever-present "why" dominates their lives. The inevitable answer is found in their cultural identity. As Jews they have been "chosen to suffer." Escape is impossible and ultimately undesirable. Flight—geographic, psychological—fails to result in a "new life." The Jewish victim, burdened by tradition, by time, and a history of suffering, must accept Abraham's covenant with God. When Malamud's victims assume responsibility for their past, they are reborn. The "new life," paradoxically, is found in the old.

In contrast, Wright's rebels, also lonely, alienated individuals, seek affirmation in action. Passion, impulsiveness, and often violence characterize many of Wright's protagonists. Most are nonreflective[12] and unable to articulate their agony. Driven by explosive emotions, they seek escape in alcohol, sex, and brutal encounters. Some leave the repressive South for the "promised land." Movement from town to city, job to job is common. Family and friends disperse; new alliances are formed but inevitably nothing changes. Disenchantment grows, finally erupting in violence. Meaning is found not in the past, but in the present. The rebel's identity depends on action. "The immediate, the spontaneous, the dangerous, the unknown . . . the active,"[13] frees the rebel and gives significance to his life. Wright's rebels feel most exhilarated, most alive when they have taken life.

Both rebels and victims seem impotent, unable to direct their destiny. Their reponses represent attempts to control their own lives. But neither are entirely free; both have been molded by history, their actions partially determined by disparate traditions. Malamud's morality, Wright's nihilism largely reflect the Jewish and Negro experiences. Their best, most representative writings are firmly rooted in their respective traditions. Wright's strongest fiction, written before he left the United States, deals with the problems of lower class Southern and Northern Negroes.[14] Likewise, "the best of Malamud's novels and stories willfully cultivate attitudes and backgrounds which are specifically Jewish . . . and which often represent a return to conditions long past."[15] Even the "nonethnic" works of Malamud and Wright fit the patterns of their more traditional fiction.[16] This study, however, emphasizes those works which focus on the problems and responses of the Jewish victim and black rebel. No attempt is made to analyze all of the authors' fiction.

Individual chapters are organized thematically. The behavior of rebels and victims are examined in the first chapter. Attitudes toward cultural identity, tradition, and religion are investigated in chapter 2; family relationships, sexual and romantic involvement in chapter 3; the shifting environments of rebel and victim in chapter 4. The final chapter explores relationships between Negroes and Jews in Wright's and Malamud's fiction.

1

Rebels and Victims

If you act at all, it is either to flee or to kill; you are either a victim or a rebel.
Richard Wright, *Twelve Million Black Voices*

Suffering is what brings us towards happiness.
Bernard Malamud, *The Natural*

Traditionally, Jews and Negroes have been considered brothers in misery, helpless victims of brutal societies. Memories of exile, pogroms, and "the final solution" cross the Atlantic to appear in works by Saul Bellow, Bernard Malamud, and Edward Lewis Wallant. Even Bruce Jay Friedman's and Philip Roth's third generation Jewish-Americans seem paranoid and unable to escape their European past. Similarly, an oppressive history haunts Afro-American literature. From William Wells Brown's nineteenth-century *Clotel* to Claude Brown's contemporary *Manchild in the Promised Land,* Negroes struggle to overcome the effects of slavery and Jim Crowism in their native land. Persecution, pain, and suffering, then, are common ingredients in Afro-American and Jewish-American literature. Yet, despite these similarities, despite the familiar preoccupation with the oppressed, contemporary Afro-American and Jewish-American literature seem quite different from each other.

Studies of Jewish fiction generally emphasize its compassionate and humanistic values; in contrast, analyses of black literature center on its rage and violence.[1] In a provocative essay, "Negroes and Jews: An Encounter in America," Leslie Fiedler notes the transformation of the Negro from "Uncle Tom into Bigger Thomas,"[2] from the pitiable nigger into the angry warrior. A similar theme runs through Addison Gayle, Jr.'s *The Way of the New World: The Black Novel in America.* Fiedler and Gayle are quite correct. No one can miss the anger and impatience in *Captain Blackman, And Then We Heard the Thunder,* or *The System of Dante's Hell.* Unwilling to appease whites, contemporary black writers reject literary ancestors like William Wells Brown, James Weldon Johnson, and Charles Chesnutt, who "shape their stories to suit a white audience."[3] In comparison with Jewish works which preach compassion and celebrate life, the tone of much recent black writing is resentful and often inflammatory. Yet, in the hands of Imamu Baraka or John A. Williams, violence has become redemptive, a necessary act of affirmation. The descendants of Richard Wright, father of the violent black protest tradition, cannot appreciate I. B. Singer's and Bernard Malamud's patient, long suffering Jews. In turn, Jewish-American writers cannot condone "the new Negro," the aggressive, militant black who rejects the commandment "Thou Shalt Not Kill."

A common concern for the victim's fate has led black and Jewish writers in different directions. How and why this has happened is revealed partially through a comparison of Richard Wright's and Bernard Malamud's fiction. Both authors raise similar questions. How should individuals respond to a cruel or indifferent environment? How can the poor and powerless survive with dignity in modern society? Their answers are quite different. While most of Malamud's protagonists emerge as victims, prepared to sacrifice and suffer for others, Wright's Negroes develop into rebels who violently attack society. Such divergent responses reflect distinctive traditions (examined in chapter 2), but they also reveal the range of options available to Negroes and Jews.

With few exceptions Wright's protagonists are passive actors in naturalistic dramas. Wright in *Black Boy,* Carl Owens in "Man of All Work," and the protagonist in "Big Black Good Man," retain their humanity, but most are not so fortunate. Saul Saunders in "The Man Who Killed A Shadow" and Bigger Thomas in *Native Son* are more typical of Wright's desperate characters who are deprived of formal education, dignified labor, and a feeling of their own worth. Even the few who are educated or have money, like Cross Damon (*The Outsider*) or Tyree Tucker (*The Long Dream*), share Bigger's frustration. Only when whites provoke them do Wright's Negroes have a chance to assert themselves. Violent rebellion allows the invisible to be seen, the inarticulate to express themselves. No longer are emotions repressed, expressions disguised, thoughts or behavior inhibited. The masks are dropped. Shuffling, downtrodden Sambos are replaced by black warriors determined to "kill as many [whites] as they can (*Uncle Tom's Children*, p. 44) in order to make their suffering meaningful.

A rising tide of violence characterizes Wright's fiction from *Uncle Tom's Children*, an early collection of short stories, to *Native Son* and *The Outsider*. The gentle Mr. Mann gives way to the violent Bigger Thomas and Cross Damon. Depicted as innocent victims of an oppressive society, the rebels appear justified in their actions. Remorse is rarely shown. Instead they exult in their newly acquired dignity and power. Though some of Wright's characters (generally women and older men) remain victims, and a few like the Reverend Taylor and Fishbelly Tucker resist nonviolently, brutal rebels dominate Wright's fiction.

Unlike Wright's Negroes, most of Malamud's Jews and non-Jews are not "the mere passive victims of social cruelty and neglect."[4] While most of Wright's people are simple, uneducated folk—tenant farmers, manual laborers, and domestics—Malamud's characters range from craftsmen and small shopkeepers to artists, writers, and teachers. At best, "lucky" Negroes like Cross Damon (*The Outsider*) and Jake Jackson (*Lawd Today*) can look forward to monotonous post office jobs, the top of Wright's occupational hierarchy, or middle class existence dependent on exploiting other blacks as Tyree Tucker does. In contrast, Malamud's protagonists are educated and usually self-employed. With the exception of *The Fixer*'s Yakov Bok, a victim of Russian anti-Semitism, they could prosper if they made compromises. But usually they are unwilling or incapable of that. In *The Assistant* Frank Alpine is free to leave Bober's decrepit grocery store for a college education or a better job, but he doesn't. In *A New Life* Seymour Levin loses his position at Cascadia College because he refuses to conform politically and socially. Even in *The Fixer,* where Russia limits Jewish freedom, Yakov Bok assumes partial responsibility for his predicament. Excluding Bok and a few Jewish refugees, Malamud's characters are not persecuted for ethnic or religious reasons. In fact, some greedy, insensitive individuals like the Karps and Pearls in *The Assistant* succeed in America. Although the environment can be cruel to Malamud's victims, their suffering is as much a consequence of their own decisions as of their bad luck.

Not that they are masochists. Like Wright's Negroes, they want some peace and happiness. Levin wants to be a good teacher; Bok dreams of being wealthy; Arthur Fidelman (*Pictures of Fidelman*) seeks to be a successful artist, while Harry Lesser (*The Tenants*) strives to finish his novel. Although their ambitions are greater than those of Wright's characters, whose dreams reflect their limited opportunities, they are not impossible fantasies. Why do most of Malamud's characters ultimately choose to sacrifice material rewards for moral obligations? In part because prosperity depends on exploiting others, which inevitably results in guilt. Also the victims' suffering is meaningful; their sacrifices become an effective weapon for change.

Resigned to his threadbare existence, Morris Bober makes life easier for his impoverished customers and sets an example for Frank, his neurotic assistant, who will in turn help others. On a grander scale, Seymour Levin succeeds in liberalizing Cascadia College's curriculum and winning allies among the cautious faculty. Unlike Leo Duffy, his unstable predecessor who commits suicide after he is fired, Levin survives. Imprisoned and tortured continually in tzarist Russia, Yakov Bok maintains his innocence, demands due process, and effectively threatens the government by winning support for his efforts. While the victories are incomplete, the victims are ennobled by their sacrifice and encouraged to continue living. Unlike most of Wright's rebels Malamud's characters generally become reformers, not revolutionaries. They use conversation, teaching, and writing to improve but not to destroy the system. More importantly, they are transformed and emerge as better people. Bok (as will later be shown) resembles Wright's rebels more than any others of Malamud's characters do, but even he relies on verbal and legal means to accomplish his goals. When Malamud's victims cry out, they are heard. Mistrusted and even feared (as Levin and Bok are), they are never ignored like Wright's Negroes, who are treated as unfeeling beasts of burden.

"Perhaps it would be possible," Wright theorizes, "for the Negro to become reconciled to his plight if he could be made to believe that his sufferings were for some remote, high sacrificial end" (*Eight Men,* p. 222). Of course, this was not possible as Wright repeatedly illustrated. In an autobiographical story, "The Man Who Went To Chicago," he described his experiences as an assistant to a

Jewish doctor who quieted the laboratory dogs by slitting their vocal chords. The image of tortured animals raising their heads in mute anguish is symbolic of Wright's "dumb niggers" who have been deprived of speech and an audience. Cut off from their folk tradition and deprived of an "adequate education,"[5] urban blacks like Bigger Thomas and Jake Jackson lack language to express suffering which even they do not understand. Instead their "hunger for expression finds its form in . . . wild, raw music . . . , in colorful dress . . . and the invention of slang" (*Twelve Million Black Voices*) designed to disguise their fear.

Rarely does language serve them as it does Malamud's characters who use it as a medium of love and friendship, as a bond with their people and their past. " 'You'll never know what your letters meant to me,' " Olga tells Mitka, a fellow writer in "The Girl of My Dreams" (*The Magic Barrel*, p. 40). " 'You can't eat language but it eases thirst,' " Harry Lesser observes in *The Tenants* (p. 13). Words are oxygen and water to Malamud's victims. Without them, life is intolerable. " 'It's hard to live without another soul to talk to,' " Yakov Bok complains after the Russians have put him in solitary. " 'How is one to ease his heart a little?' " (*The Fixer*, p. 188). Through language, the written and spoken word, Malamud's characters "ease their hearts." Bok maintains his sanity by devouring the printed page. Newspaper scraps, Old Testament passages, and even the Gospels sustain him. "Hung[ry] . . . for words" (p. 230), he scrutinizes a little scroll from a phylactery (a small leather box containing quotations from the Hebrew Scriptures) and dreams of communicating with another person. When a new prisoner in an adjacent cell taps on the wall, he responds eagerly and despairs at the sound of silence. Similarly, Frank Alpine (*The Assistant*) seeks relief by sharing his unhappy past with Morris Bober, the empathetic Jewish grocer, and his sensitive daughter Helen. Deprived of their friendship and conversation, he finds life unbearable.

Wright's characters also need to express themselves. When Bigger Thomas finally begins to comprehend his life, he gropes for words, trying to communicate his agony to Max, his lawyer. But the words which flow eloquently and easily from the Jewish lawyer elude Bigger, and one is again reminded of the devocalized dogs yowling in silence. Even Wright's articulate Negroes appear dumb, for if they possess the vocabulary, they have been trained to conceal their emotions from whites and from other blacks. Thus, Tyree Tucker, the wealthy black businessman in *The Long Dream,* guards his words, speaks in whispers, and teaches his son to do the same. Forced to dissemble before white officials, neither Tyree nor his son Fish can reconcile their emotions, their words, and their actions. Words, then, become meaningless and untrustworthy as Fish realizes when his father, cowering in front of white vigilantes, tells him to " 'be a man' " (p. 66). Dependent on whites for survival, the Tuckers must not appear too intelligent or "uppity." With exaggerated subservience and false gaiety, Tyree disguises his anger in front of whites.

Ultimately, role playing warps Wright's Negroes, stunting their personalities and preventing them from developing intimate, trusting relationships. Emotionally numb, they live in an "unreal shadowy world" (*Eight Men,* p. 194), as Saul Saunders does in "The Man Who Killed A Shadow," a shortened version of *Native Son.* Like Bigger, he too cannot relate to anyone since "people never really become personalities to him" (p. 194). With more intelligence and education Saul could be Cross Damon, the cool, detached outsider, conscious of his suffering but unable to express it to other blacks. Unlike many of Wright's characters, Damon, an avid reader with a college background, possesses the understanding and vocabulary essential for communication, but he lacks a sympathetic listener until he meets Ely Houston, a hunchbacked white district attorney. Despite the fact that Damon, a murderer, must guard himself, he feels closer to Houston (himself an outsider because of his deformity) than to any Negroes.

Wright's protagonists, like Malamud's, have a need to communicate their suffering, but they are denied relief. When they find the words and cry out, they are not heard. In "The Man Who Lived Underground," a story resembling The Book of Daniel, Dostoievsky's "Notes from the Underground," and Ellison's *Invisible Man,* Fred Daniels discovers the meaning of his life while a fugitive in a sewer. From his underground asylum, he breaks into several stores and takes money, guns, and other objects. Initially he delights in the white world's possessions and the sense of power they temporarily offer, but gradually he realizes the paltriness of the life they represent. When he attempts to share his insights with a Negro congregation, they dismiss him as a lunatic. Desperate for an audience, he surrenders and reveals his activities to the police who first mock and then kill him. " 'You've got to shoot his kind. They'd wreck things" (*Eight Men*, p. 92), responds Officer Lawson when asked why he murdered Daniels.

Scorned by whites and feared by slavish Negroes, the rebels are truly outsiders whose only recourse appears to be violence. Even the successful Wright, who learned to use words as a weapon, was capable of brutality. In the autobiographical *Black Boy*, the author, a young boy, rebels against his authoritarian father by killing an innocent kitten. The animal had disturbed Wright, Sr.'s sleep, and unthinkingly he had told his son to get rid of it. Though Richard realized that his father was speaking figuratively, he enacted the command and reflected that "deep hate of [his father] urged him toward a literal acceptance of his word" (p. 10).

Detailed gory descriptions of animal slaughter are common in Wright's fiction. In "Big Boy Leaves Home" the protagonist strangles a snake and a dog. *Native Son* begins with Bigger sadistically destroying a rat. Saul Saunders enjoys his brief employment as an exterminator of "rats, mice and roaches" (p. 197). Often animal butchery is a prelude or postlude to murdering people. In "Big Boy Leaves Home" it occurs shortly after a white man is shot. In "The Man Who Killed A Shadow" and in *Native Son*, it foreshadows confrontations with whites. But in all instances the acts integrate self-defense and release of rage as do the murders of people. Richard kills the kitten to protect himself from his father's wrath but also to "hit back at him" (*Black Boy*, p. 10). Big Boy destroys the animals to protect his hiding place and to discharge his fear. Though Saul supports himself as an exterminator, the work is also emotionally rewarding. His comment, "he never felt better in his life than when he was killing with the sanction of society" (p. 198), reveals a deep need for violent expression and is applicable to both Richard Wright and Bigger Thomas. Bigger has his family's gratitude when he defends them, but his prolonged playing with the rodent indicates that he is satisfying his own needs. Young Richard justifies his action by saying, " 'now papa can sleep' " (p. 10), but he knows that that is not the real motivation. Like the others' violence, his killing has been sanctioned, and Wright anticipates enjoyment in using his father's rash words in his own defense. By destroying the animals, Wright and his characters can express their anger safely and retaliate vicariously against the enemy.

By contrast, Malamud's protagonists regard animals and birds as a sacred part of life. Instead of the vermin, rodents, and snakes which populate Wright's fiction and are identified with corrupt humanity, horses, cows, cats, and birds appear in Malamud's works and are viewed as companions. Instead of killing a kitten, Bok begs for one to keep him company in jail. In *The Assistant* Frank Alpine admires St. Francis's ability to preach to the birds and to sacrifice for the poor. As he gradually assumes responsibility for the Bober family, he begins to resemble a fragile bird. "He grows thin, his neck scrawny, face bones prominent, his broken nose sharp" (p. 241). In *A New Life* Duffy, who kills himself, is described as a "proud bird [who] had flown his coop" (p. 337). Obviously, Malamud's birds and people are earthbound. Unable to escape their troubles by soaring to great heights, they depend on crumbs of compassion to sustain them. In a surrealistic story—"The Jewbird"—identification between man and fowl is complete when Schwartz, an aging, weary black bird symbolizing the suffering Jews, moves in with Harry Cohen who initially tolerates him for his son's sake, but finally beats him and throws him out. Like the ancient mariner and Yakov Bok, Schwartz has a "desperate desire to make known his fate" (*The Fixer,* p. 160). But he has chosen the wrong household, for Cohen (ironically a name reserved for Jewish high priests) is no better than the "anti-semeets" (*Idiots First,* p. 113) harassing Schwartz. Although the demanding Jewbird is somewhat of a nuisance, he does not deserve to die. Cohen's actions are reprehensible, a sign of man's inhumanity to man.

Most of Malamud's protagonists, however, are not Cohens. Even in self-defense they hesitate to hurt animals. Confronted by a wild dog, Levin is immobilized and earns his date's contempt because she must drive it away. Partly he is afraid "to antagonize" (p. 84), but he is also unwilling to inflict pain. Later Levin considers hurling a rock at a mule obstructing the road but instead tries charming it with candy and ferns. Not surprisingly, the method fails; only when he accidentally blasts the car horn does the animal move. Despite such evidence that force works, Malamud's victims resist using it.

Occasionally when they ignore their consciences, they suffer terribly. In *The Fixer* Yakov Bok's destiny is intertwined with the fate of his horse. Despite misgivings, he sells the nag to an anti-Semitic boatman who ferries him across the river. As Bok glances back at the horse "tethered to a paling" he reflects that the animal looks "like an old Jew" (p. 27). The image is significant, for later the fixer will find himself imprisoned, chained to the wall, a "bag of old bones" (p. 26), unable to move. At one point Bok's feet become infected and he is forced to crawl "like a dog" (p. 185) to the prison infirmary. The other inmates jeer and compare him to a "Zhid mule" (p. 185). Haunted by the past, Bok recalls all the sins he had committed—against his wife, his father-in-law, and his horse. While his family visits him in jail and forgives him, the dead horse appears in his nightmares and labels him a " 'murderer! a horsekiller! You deserve what you get' " (p. 249), the horse, his conscience, tells him.

"Talking Horse," a more recent short story, further emphasizes the holiness of all life. The protagonist, Abramovitz, has the body of an animal and the spirit of a man. Like the Jewbird, he is treated callously by his master, Goldberg, a deaf-mute who resembles Cohen and Wright's rebels, brutal men of few words. More fortunate, however, than the talking bird, Abramovitz struggles and succeeds in freeing himself. In a final mad melee, he strikes Goldberg who inadvertantly acts as a midwife, delivering a man's head. Now a centaur, Abramovitz gallops off to freedom (*Rembrandt's Hat,* pp. 177–204). The message in this and other Malamudian tales is clear. Appearances can be deceptive. Essence, not form, distinguishes men from animals. A reverence for freedom and life defines what is human.

The absence of freedom provokes Wright's rebels to attack family and friends, sometimes in self-defense, sometimes in anger and hatred. *Black Boy* serves as a partial model for Wright's other works in which protagonists reflect their brutal environments. Although Richard never raised his hands to his mother, he defended himself with a kitchen knife and razor blades against his Aunt Addie's and Uncle Tom's attempts to "break [his] spirit" (*Black Boy,* p. 140). Fights at Negro schools and in black neighborhoods were more common than the interracial battle described in "Living Ethics of Jim Crow." Unlike his characters, Wright did not enjoy such encounters and only participated to protect his life and maintain his honor. He blamed whites for pitting blacks against each other. In one horrifying scene, Wright and Harrison, a black co-worker, are urged to box each other for the white employees' pleasure. Although they agree to fake it, the fight escalates into a "battle royal," anticipating the famous episode in *Invisible Man.* Like Ellison, Wright accuses whites of manipulating and controlling black behavior and emotions, of destroying Negro fellowship. "The shame and anger we felt," he writes in *Black Boy*, "for having allowed ourselves to be duped crept into our blows. . . . The hate we felt for the [white] man . . . went into the blows we threw at each other" (p. 212).

Such displaced rage warps most black friendships. Beneath the superficial camaraderie seethes hostility and suspicion. At any time "playing the dozens" (verbal one-upmanship) and frisky wrestling can erupt into violence foreshadowing conflicts with whites. In "Big Boy Leaves Home" a romp in the woods ends disastrously as the protagonist, asserting his masculinity, nearly breaks his friend's neck, and shortly after shoots a white man in anger and in self-defense. Terrified of robbing a white shopkeeper, Bigger Thomas sublimates his fear by first killing a rat and then viciously attacking his friend Gus, who senses his dread. A similar pattern exists in *The Outsider* when Cross Damon first kills Joe, a black co-worker, and later murders three whites. By first attacking less formidable black targets, Wright's rebels are emboldened to assail white oppressors. Such internecine warfare is inevitable when self-hatred flourishes and frustration has no outlet.

In *The Long Dream* Fishbelly Tucker, who resembles young Wright, also recognizes suicidal tendencies in black communities. Visiting a "hit the nigger head" booth at a local fair, Fish and his friends are encouraged by white onlookers to attack the nigger head. In a scene reminiscent of the Wright-Harrison fight, the youths comply, bombarding their own image and increasing their own self-hatred. In another episode they taunt and assault Aggie, an effeminate black boy who they feel threatens their masculinity. Sensitive and compassionate, Fish is troubled by his behavior. He realizes that "to quell the war in his heart, he had either to reject [the nigger head] in hate or accept it in love." Since "it was easier to hate that degraded black face than to love it" (p. 46), he flees America to avoid being killed or becoming a killer. In Wright's view Fish has little choice. "If [he] acts at all, it is either to flee or to kill; [he is] either a victim or a rebel" (*Twelve Million Voices*, p. 57). There is no possibility that he can remain imprisoned and survive with dignity as Malamud's victims do. However, he is more fortunate than many of Wright's characters. Reinforced by his parents' love and money, he escapes to France.

For most of Wright's protagonists the only alternative is violent rebellion if they are to replace self-contempt with self-respect. Persecuted for years, they become powder kegs of rage waiting to be ignited. The pattern is established in *Uncle Tom's Children,* Southern tales depicting the development of Negro victim into black rebel. The seeds of Northern defiance are planted in the South where a gentle minister helplessly watches his congregation starve; a Negro woman is beaten while trying to protect her son; a hard working farmer discovers that his wife is "fair game" for whites; and a Negro youth witnesses his friends' brutal murder and mutilation. Two of the stories—"Fire and Cloud" and "Bright and Morning Star"—written during Wright's communist period, suggest radical political action as a possible solution for the Negro's troubles, but they are not representative of the collection, which pits individual blacks against villainous whites. The Reverend Taylor in "Fire and Cloud" and Aunt Sue in "Bright and Morning Star" resemble Yakov Bok who learns that " 'there's no such thing as an unpolitical man. . . . You can't sit still and see yourself destroyed' " (*The Fixer,* p. 335). Beaten by whites who fear his concern for his congregation, Taylor experiences a "symbolic baptism in fire and blood"[6] which transforms him as torture has changed Yakov Bok. At the story's end, the minister combines prayer with marching, religion with politics as he joins two Communists in leading poor blacks and whites in a successful demonstration for food.

Such interracial cooperation and nonviolent tactics are not effective, however, in "Bright and Morning Star" in which Booker, a white party member, betrays Aunt Sue, her son John, and other black Communists. Although Sue loves Reva, John's white girlfriend, she hates other whites and with good reason. Booker abuses her confidence; the sheriff and his men beat and humiliate her; a white mob looks on as John is tortured. As in most of Wright's fiction, whites loom as a hard, immovable "mountain" (p. 213) dominating black life. Only the heat of black anger, and the fire of black weapons can penetrate the cold white world and loosen its grip on the Negro community. When Sue openly defies the white mob by shooting Booker, she gains peace, but she pays with her life as do most of Wright's protagonists.

No matter how hard they try, Wright's Negroes cannot escape white tyranny. The "white mountain" demands continuous sacrifice so that even those who accommodate it eventually must choose between a humiliating existence and a dignified death. In "Long Black Song" Silas, a hardworking farmer, discovers his wife has slept with a white traveling salesman. His actions follow a predictable pattern. Having beaten her, Silas assaults the salesman who callously has returned to collect money for his merchandise. Unable to whip him, he races for his gun and is transformed when he kills the white man. "His voice was hard and cold. . . . It was as though he had gone far off and had stayed a long time and had come back changed" (p. 123). The discovery of his wife's treachery, of the white man's power, of his own impotency, strips Silas of any illusions that he can control his life. Only violence can redeem his self-respect. Like Aunt Sue he decides " 'to be hard like they is!' " (p. 125). But at least, he reasons, he has one choice left. He can "kill as many as" possible (p. 128) and determine the manner of his death. The last scene is a "baptism in fire and blood" as Silas exchanges shots with the white posse and is trapped in his burning house. The scorched earth and dead white bodies testify to the depth of black rage.

In "Big Boy Leaves Home" the protagonist responds similarly when he inadvertently frightens a white woman near the creek where he and his friends have been swimming nude. Determined to get his clothes, Big Boy advances steadily towards the woman whose outraged boyfriend shoots two of the black boys. At the sight of his dead friends, Big Boy is overwhelmed by anger; swiftly the victim gives way to the rebel. Assuming control, he wrests the rifle from the white man, fires, and destroys the symbol of his oppression. " 'Ahll kill yuh; ahll kill yuh' " (p. 29), he repeats. All his energy and will are directed towards this momentous release. The violent moment is a climax in Big Boy's life as it is in the lives of Wright's other rebels. Later, hiding in a pit, he observes the tarring, feathering, and burning of Bobo, another friend. As the flames leap higher, they sear Big Boy's consciousness and fan his hate. Only the fantasy of killing many white men comforts him. He smiles bitterly, thinking of the newspaper headlines reporting his actions.

In the North Big Boy will harden into Bigger Thomas, *Native Son*'s semiliterate, brutal, slum youth who menaces both blacks and whites. Unlike Aunt Sue, the Reverend Taylor, and Silas, Bigger has nothing—no ambitions, political commitment, vocation, family, or community loyalty. Even more desperate than the characters in

Uncle Tom's Children and *The Long Dream,* he struggles to contain his fear and anger, repressing his emotions and establishing a "wall, a curtain" between himself and others. Afraid of "kill[ing] himself or someone else" (*Native Son,* p. 9), he blots out his surroundings and seeks relief through drinking, fornicating, and brawling. Like a wounded animal, Bigger is dangerous. One taste of blood can unleash savage instincts revealed in the opening scene, which, as Robert Bone observes, foreshadows "the whole novel."[7] The pleasure Bigger derives from crushing the rat's skull anticipates his response to the murders of Mary Dalton, a white woman, and Bessie, his black girlfriend. Although the first killing is accidental and the second is committed hesitatingly, afterwards he feels exhilarated, alive for the first time. In both cases the women's heads are crushed as the rat's skull is. If, as Frantz Fanon suggests, the Jew symbolizes the intellectual threat to society, then Bigger, the "savage nigger," represents the biological threat.[8] Since white America has stunted his intellectual and emotional development, he responds in kind, destroying his victims' brains, the potential source of such growth.

Ironically, Northern liberalism, not Southern brutality, provokes black rebellion. The novel condemns the hypocritical Daltons, wealthy slum landlords who assuage their consciences by "adopting" Negroes, feeding, employing, and educating them in return for affection and loyalty. Ignorant of Bigger's needs and feelings, they treat him as a house pet; but he is not their faithful white cat. Distrusting, defensive, and tough, he is a black alley "tom," wary of his new employers, of Mr. Dalton's persistent questions, of Mrs. Dalton's charity, and of their daughter Mary's superficial radicalism. Instead of feeling grateful, he feels impotent, overwhelmed by the "white mountain that looms over him" (p. 350). When Mary and Jan Erlone, her Communist boyfriend, pressure him into visiting a soul food restaurant, he sees himself as an object of amusement and responds with "a dumb, cold and inarticulate hate" (p. 58). Later, after an evening of drinking, he is forced to escort the drunken girl to her bedroom where, torn between desire and hate, he caresses her and then panicking, smothers her when Mrs. Dalton gropingly enters the room. Although Mary's death is accidental, Bigger realizes that he has "murdered many times in his heart" (p. 90). The scene with the semiconscious girl and her blind mother emphasizes Bigger's invisibility and underscores white myopia in dealing with blacks. Wright clearly blames white Americans for creating a creature so hurt and hopeless that only violence provides fulfillment. Bigger feels no regret, only pride that "he ha[s] murdered and created a new life for himself" (p. 90). His pride is reinforced when he successfully outwits the white authorities by playing the "dumb nigger," a role which allows him to survive. Having killed a white person, he hesitates only briefly before murdering his girlfriend Bessie, who threatens his freedom, and throwing her body out the window.

The attention denied Bigger is shortly his as he becomes the object of a massive manhunt. In a climactic scene, Bigger, trapped on a rooftop, reacts like Wright's other rebels. Refusing to surrender, he satisfies Big Boy's fantasy as he crushes an officer's skull, shoots wildly at the others, and becomes an overnight "celebrity" in the press. Captured and imprisoned, Bigger, like Bok, loses his fear of death. But unlike Bok, who gains some Jewish and Russian support, Bigger horrifies blacks and whites and repels his own lawyer. At the end of Malamud's novel the prison doors open and the fixer emerges as a Jewish spokesman. At the close of *Native Son* the doors clang shut, and Bigger, unable to communicate with Max, is left alone. Not surprisingly, his fate differs from Bok's since he, like Cross Damon, "has lived outside of the lives of men. Their modes of communication, their symbols and images [have] been denied him," (p. 353) and he, in turn, has denied them. Bigger dies as he has lived—alone—but with an understanding of his suffering.

Native Son serves as Wright's warning to white America to recognize her invisible sons before they ruthlessly judge and condemn their country. With nothing to live for, his characters are willing to die for freedom. The more intelligent and sensitive they are, the more they threaten society, as Cross Damon proves when a sense of powerlessness drives him to play God in *The Outsider*. Despite Wright's insistence that race is only incidental to the novel, evidence indicates otherwise. "Damon's crimes were part and parcel of the everyday life of man, most particularly Black men."[9] What distinguishes Damon from Wright's other black rebels is his philosophical temperament, his tendency to analyze his actions. In other respects he fits the tradition of Wright's persecuted protagonists. Though well educated, he is frustrated and, like Jake Jackson in *Lawd Today*, locked into a monotonous, demeaning post office job and an unhappy marriage. Actually, the first part of *The Outsider* is borrowed from

Lawd Today.[10] Financially dependent on his white employers, Cross Damon must conceal his anger and endure lectures about irresponsible "niggers." Only by pretending to be a "coon clown"(*The Outsider,* p. 145) can he falsify records and change his name. Although he lies and kills, he is able to deceive the Communists and Eva, his white girlfriend, by acting naive and innocent. In fact, the whole novel focuses on his role playing, his attempt to take advantage of a train wreck and assume a new identity in New York. But Cross can no more change his behavior and escape his problem than Bigger can.

Intended as an existential hero of any race, he is really a "vicious, angry . . . intellectual version of [the primitive] Bigger Thomas."[11] Both manipulate people in order to feel powerful. While one dangles a rat before his terrified sister, the other watches people scramble for the coins he drops from windows. Fleeing the poverty and hopelessness of a Chicago slum, Cross behaves like Bigger. "With the speed of a panther" (p. 99), he kills Joe, a black co-worker who threatens his new life, and dumps him out the window (as Bigger does to his girlfriend Bessie). The violence continues in New York where he becomes embroiled with several demagogues, a Fascist and two Communists, whom he murders, partly to avenge his black friends "but mainly to rid himself of . . . their assumption that [they] could have made a slave of him" (p. 280). As in *Native Son,* the victims' skulls are crushed, and although the homicides are unplanned, they are cooly executed and concealed, without any evidence of remorse. Furthermore, Damon is able to outwit the Communists and the authorities just as Bigger misleads the Daltons and the police.

In both novels whites are cast as villains, but there are the exceptional few who are presented sympathetically. In *Native Son* Mr. Max and Jan Erlone, committed Communists, undertake Bigger's defense; in *The Outsider* Cross becomes involved with Eva, a frail white girl, and Ely Houston, a hunchbacked district attorney. All interracial relationships are doomed to failure, however. For although Damon is more intelligent and articulate than Bigger, he is also black and a criminal. Neither Eva nor Ely regard him as an equal. The former, a naive version of Reva in "Bright and Morning Star," views him as a poor black victim deserving pity which she confuses with love. As long as she considers him exploited like herself, she feels secure, but when the truth is revealed, she commits suicide, a victim of the rebel's violence as much as Bessie is. Even Damon's friendship with Houston underscores the importance of race in the novel. The district attorney first takes an interest in him because "he has never had a chance to talk to Negroes as he'd like to . . . [and he finds them] hypnotizing" (p. 122). Although Houston, a cripple, considers himself a fellow outsider, he has more in common with Mr. Max, the Jewish lawyer who comforts his client by telling him that Jews and Communists are also persecuted. But like Bigger, Cross knows that Negroes especially are singled out and hated, even though he insists that "color . . . consciousness" (p. 131) had not influenced his actions. When the D.A. suggests that as outsiders "Negroes will develop unique and specially defined psychological types," he appreciates "the aptness of the remarks" (p. 119). While the physically deformed Houston is chosen to enforce the law, the racially scarred black outsider must operate beyond the law to be free. If race is incidental, why aren't the roles reversed? The answer is obvious. Wright drew upon reality when he cast the Negro as rebel, the white man as his judge. This reality condemns his black protagonists to fearful "shadowy" existences until they rebel and discover meaning in their suffering, purpose in their lives. Violence, particularly against whites, is affirmed because other options deny the self and subdue the black man, making him invisible, a condition the rebels reject, preferring "to die without shame" if they cannot live with pride.

While death provides the only honorable alternative for Wright's rebels, it is shunned by most of Malamud's characters, who acquire self-respect, recognition, and even influence when they assume responsibility for others (an obvious exception, *The Tenants,* is discussed in later chapters). Despite their bleak environments, they still possess their own humanitarian values. Not that they are saints; they make mistakes, but their consciences demand that they atone if they are to "find peace of mind" (*Pictures of Fidelman,* p. 20). Frequently Malamud's victims choose between the lesser of evils. Thus, Morris Bober, the impoverished, aging grocer in *The Assistant,* sacrifices material prosperity and his family's comfort because he cannot exploit others. Bober even berates himself for envying his neighbors' success and for wishing them ill. When Schmitz, a business competitor, becomes sick, the grocer, in a Jewish act of contrition, "severely [strikes] his chest" (p. 80). Similarly, his conscience will not allow him to unload the store on an unsuspecting refugee whom he pities. When he halfheartedly tries to burn the store down for insurance, his hand shakes and he sets himself on fire instead. As Malamud's quintessential "schlemiel," the grocer partially shapes his fate and "has a hand in his own destruction."[12] He trusts a partner who "juggles the books," an assistant who steals from his cash register, and customers who default on their bills. Given a choice between hurting themselves or others, Wright's rebels choose the latter, Malamud's victims the former.

The losers in Malamud's fiction are not the poor and humble, but the self-centered and greedy. In "The Bill" Willy Schlegal despises himself for failing to repay Panessa, the impoverished storekeeper who dies from neglect. The guilt-ridden janitor resembles the corpse being buried: "his tongue hung in his mouth like dead fruit on a tree, and his heart was a black-painted window" (*The Magic Barrel,* p. 153). In Malamud's arsenal selfishness, indifference, and dishonesty are as deadly as the guns in Wright's stories. They take lives, destroy friendships, and debase individuals. In "The Loan" Lieb, a successful baker, obeys his wife and denies an old friend money. Although Kobotsky, a "schnorrer,"[13] had taken advantage of him before, Lieb feels guilty about withholding help, and as punishment his famous breads burn. Likened to "charred corpses" (p. 191), they represent the denial of "the staff of life," the death of friendship, and the destruction of six million Jews, abandoned by indifferent countrymen to the ovens at Dachau and Aushwitz.

In *Pictures of Fidelman* obligation to others is stressed again. " 'You are responsible [for me]' " (p. 16), Susskind, a Jewish refugee informs Arthur Fidelman, a would-be artist, who degenerates when he ignores the Malamudian first commandment. A series of short stories, *Pictures of Fidelman* chronicles the degradation of art and artist as the latter places work before love, self before others. Just as Lieb's breads burn, Fidelman's art decays—evidence of its creator's sins. Driven by vanity, he disregards his mistress's pleas to complete his painting and marry her. Instead, listening to Ludovico, a satanic alter ego, he adds "finishing touches" which ruin the work and his life. Filled with self-disgust, he blackens the canvas, thereby burying his creation and provoking Esmeralda who "comes at him with the bread knife" (p. 147). A typical "schlemiel," Fidelman "plunges it into his gut," and utters the victim's epitaph, " 'this serves me right' " (p. 147).

Fidelman, however, has not yet learned Susskind's (and Malamud's) lesson and must sink further before he is redeemed. In the next tale—"Pictures of an Artist"—his moral disintegration is completed. Having obeyed the devil within, he wallows in filth, "pissing in muddy waters" (p. 149) which choke him. A reflection of his life, his art depicts death and evil, "S. Denis, decapitated, . . . S. Catherine broken apart on spiked wheel, . . . S. Bartholomew flayed alive" (p. 150). Angry with the world, Fidelman resembles Wright's obsessed rebels, except that they have no choice, while he has elected to follow Ludovico rather than Susskind. Moreover, where their rebellion against society affirms their freedom, his assault on convention negates his. As a result Fidelman disintegrates. His language is fragmented; his philosophy is incoherent or platitudinous; his abstract art celebrates chaos; his soul embraces evil. He has lost the moral bearing which inspires art and infuses life with meaning. What "works" for Wright's characters cannot work for Malamud's as Fidelman discovers when a poor man whom he has cheated topples him into his own art, a "square hole in the ground" (p. 155), itself a comment on the errant artist. Like other Malamudian protagonists, he literally has dug his own grave. But resurrection is possible if he disciplines himself and accepts responsibility for others. By sacrificing his art for Beppo, a bisexual Venetian glass blower who teaches him the pain and joy of loving, Fidelman is redeemed. In the last story—"Glass Blower of Venice"—translucent glass replaces "muddy waters" when Fidelman exchanges abstract art for human involvement.

Similar options are available to Frank Alpine in *The Assistant* and Seymour Levin in *A New Life*. Weak and self-pitying, both make poor choices which threaten to bury them. Levin's tomb had been a New York cellar where "for two years [he had] lived in self-hatred, willing to part with life . . . [until] he came to believe what [he] often wanted to, that life is holy" (p. 201). Paradoxically, such knowledge both frees and burdens Malamud's victims, for it grants them power to shape their lives and makes them responsible for their actions. Thus, in contrast to Wright's characters who act impulsively and blame society, Levin, an inexperienced college instructor, agonizes over the effects of all his decisions. Has he falsely accused one student of plagiarizing? Has he graded another fairly? Should he compete for the chairmanship in order to revitalize the English Department? More importantly, what are his obligations to Pauline Gilley whom he loves and to her husband, Gerald, who has hired him? The questions demand answers which frequently elude him. The problems are complex, their resolutions not wholly satisfactory. Levin succeeds in modifying the English program and in winning Pauline, but he sacrifices his job and a career in college teaching. Furthermore, he is saddled with the pregnant Pauline he no longer loves and with her obnoxious, adopted children. In one sense he confronts a bleak future of burdens and deprivations. In another sense he is better off, for his dedication to principle has given his life purpose. Spiritual harmony is earned through physical hardship. Levin arrives in Oregon with nothing but his horrifying memories of a father who died in prison and a mother who killed herself with a bread knife. He leaves for New York with the Gilley children and their mother who "smell[ing] like fresh-baked bread" (p. 366) is a symbol of life's promise.

An even greater moral crisis confronts Frank Alpine, a penniless drifter in *The Assistant,* who is persuaded by Ward Minogue, a petty criminal, to participate in a robbery. A product of a broken home, like Levin and many of Wright's characters, Alpine has the potential, in Ihab Hassan's words, to become "saint or criminal" and to "be for [or] against all men."[14] He "whirls from lover to hater, victim to victimizer, and saint to criminal."[15] Reluctantly he helps rob Morris Bober, the saintly grocer, but feels remorseful and tries to atone by becoming his assistant. He works hard in the store but steals from the cash register. He reveals his unhappy past but lies about recent activities. He falls in love with Helen, the grocer's daughter, but spies on her in the shower and later rapes her. Through it all Alpine suffers, chastizing himself for his transgressions as Wright's rebels rarely do. His crimes torment him: "He groans, . . . feels short of breath, . . . sweat[s] profusely (p. 69), . . . and mutter[s] to himself" (p. 85). At other times "he crawls under the blanket in bed, trying to smother his thoughts, but they escape and stink" (p. 174). Like Fidelman, he is drowning in "muddy waters." And yet he continues to sin and perversely to take pleasure in it and "in his misery" (p. 69).

Like Bigger Thomas, Alpine, as his name suggests, has a need to scale great heights, to be recognized. Dissatisfied with his dreary existence, he seeks "adventure and fortune." If he cannot succeed legitimately, he will, like Bigger, become a criminal "Horatio Alger, a good little bad boy who has a dream and works it out."[16] He "shivers with pleasure as he conceives [of] violent acts helping to satisfy a craving that somebody suffer as his own fortune improved" (p. 92). Since Alpine, however, is not one of Wright's oppressed blacks, he can entertain another vision of himself as a highly disciplined, self-sacrificing individual, a disciple of St. Francis whom he has always admired. Having literally fallen into Bober's freshly dug grave, he arises renewed by his commitment to replace the grocer as guardian of his values and his women. Like Levin, he sacrifices his ambitions, his seeming self-interest for principle and the possibility of love. Yet by the novel's end, he has learned self-discipline, and his suffering has become meaningful because it serves others.

Although similar choices confront Yakov Bok in *The Fixer,* the pressure to rebel is greater. Of all of Malamud's novels *The Fixer* most closely resembles Wright's works in its depiction of an oppressive society determined to crush its minorities. Like Wright's rebels, Bok is deprived of freedom and dignity and finally driven to resist a cruel system. In a sense, he too becomes a rebel, willing to attack his Russian oppressors. But here the parallels end, for his actions are consistently nonviolent despite his dream of killing Tzar Nicholas. Not that Bok is any less persecuted than Wright's characters are. He has lost his parents in a pogrom and as a Jew is restricted to the ghetto. Unlike Bigger Thomas, he is innocent and wrongly imprisoned. Nevertheless, his rebellion is nonviolent, and he acts on behalf of all his people. Bok is Job with a twist, suffering not for God but for man, converting his pain into a weapon of defiance.

Angry and provoked like Wright's rebels, he retaliates in a different fashion. By stubbornly clinging to life and insisting on his rights, he unnerves the Russian authorities who learn that while they can violate his body they cannot destroy his spirit. In a sense, when Bigger and Cross murder, they fulfill themselves, but they also provide American racists with an excuse to persecute them. Yakov's oppressors don't understand this peculiar man who occupies himself by sweeping the cell, reading the Bible, mumbling to himself about man's nature and the importance of freedom. His stubbornness, his discipline, his fluency intimidate them. " 'Be respectful if you know what's good for you' " (p. 134) Grubeshov, the prosecuting attorney, commands Bok. But he ignores Grubeshov and complains about his aching feet, the smelly cell, the rotten, poisoned food, the numerous indignities forced upon him. His demeanor aggravates the Russian authorities. Immediately after being warned to " 'obey all rules and regulations without question,' " the fixer complains of loneliness and requests an animal for companionship. The astounded warden sputters the usual Russian anti-Semitism: " 'only you Jew prisoners have the nerve to make such requests' " (p. 188). And perhaps he is correct about the uniqueness of Jewish "chutzpah" or brashness, at least in contrast to the conduct of Wright's characters who are generally inarticulate in the presence of authority. When the latter are jailed, they appear withdrawn, even compliant, allowing others to defend them. Max becomes Bigger's spokesman in *Native Son*. Tyree Tucker arranges to free Fishbelly, his frightened son, whose fainting had amused the police. Yakov, however, speaks for himself. True, he has assistance from a just, humane Russian, Bibikov, the investigating magistrate, but from the beginning he is his own advocate, and after Bibikov is assassinated the Jew relies on his own wits to survive.

By remaining principled and demanding justice, Bok threatens the autocracy, earns the respect of fellow Jews and even of some Russians who are willing to risk their lives to help him. Bok's relationship with Bibikov illustrates the last point. The investigating magistrate agrees to defend the fixer because he believes in his innocence and shares with him a love of freedom. Long philosophical exchanges about God, religion, liberty, and Russian society seal their friendship. Bibikov likes and respects Bok, in contrast to Max who pities Bigger and defends him on abstract, ideological grounds. Since the white lawyer patronizes his poor black client, it is not surprising that their "relationship" dissolves when Bigger asserts that murder has given his life meaning. There has never been any real communication between them. Even in *The Outsider* where Cross Damon and Ely Houston are intellectually compatible, the relationship is strained, for Damon's guilt makes Houston an adversary. And though they are temperamentally closer than any other whites and blacks in Wright's fiction, there is a limit to Houston's comprehension. As Damon is dying, the district attorney gently questions him, seeking to understand his life and his motives for murder. More sensitive than Max, Houston, nevertheless, is unable to get "inside" his friend who dies an "outsider," proclaiming that despite his conduct, he feels " 'innocent' " (p. 405).

The rebels' actions and attitudes contrast starkly with the victims'. Wright's characters murder repeatedly yet feel innocent while Bok feels guilty for an act he did not commit. Imprisoned interminably, he dreams of the butchered child whose body he has been forced to see. Like Fidelman's "hole in the ground," Levin's "cellar," and Alpine's grocery, Bok's cell becomes both tomb and womb, containing the possibilities of death and life. In it he torments himself with real and imagined misdeeds against his family and community. Through suffering, he loses his fear of the corrupt system which oppresses him. When offered a pardon, he refuses, knowing it will taint him and his people with guilt. Close to death, Bok learns to appreciate life and to value the limited freedom he once had in the "shtetl." Armed with such knowledge and his innocence, he can confront the Russian state, demand a trial, and proclaim his truth to the world. He may lose his case in court, but he has gained dignity, self-respect, and purpose as an advocate for his oppressed people.

Both rebels and victims begin as outsiders with similar needs for recognition and self esteem, yet they develop quite differently. The rebels fulfill themselves through violence, the victims through suffering and sacrificing for others. In Wright's fiction the criminal is white society; the rebel is innocent and his actions are legitimate. In Malamud's works saint and sinner are often one; individuals have free will and the victim must accept responsibility for his deeds. Such divergent behavior reflects in part different environments. But it is also a consequence of distinctive histories and religious experiences, which are the subjects of the next chapter.

2

Genesis

A Chosen People is a choosing people.
                                   Israel Zangwill
Captivity under Christendom blasted our lives,
disrupted our families . . . and destroyed our very
images and symbols which had guided our minds
and feelings. . . . They extended our Christian salvation to us without granting the boon of freedom.
                    Richard Wright, "Our Strange Birth."

Religion satisfies universal needs. For the faithful it eases
pain, offers hope, and orders chaos. It comforts the poor and
persecuted and guides the lost. Understandably, then, it is an
important subject in black and Jewish literature which focuses on the
oppressed. In the eighteenth century the Negro poets Jupiter Ham-
mon and Phyllis Wheatley urged slaves to seek solace and justice in a
Christian heaven. By the nineteenth century other blacks like David
Walker and Frederick Douglass used religion to attack racism and
support equality. In the early twentieth century both viewpoints were
propounded, frequently by the same writers. Thus, some of Paul
Lawrence Dunbar's and James Weldon Johnson's works reveal an
other-wordly orientation, while others emphasize religion as an·
instrument of social change.[1] It was not until the 1920s, however, that
religion was repudiated in the works of Countee Cullen, Langston
Hughes, and Nella Larsen.[2] The new development paved the way for
Richard Wright and his literary descendants, whose condemnations
of Christianity dominate twentieth-century Afro-American literature.
    The reverse trend has occurred in Jewish-American literature.
While early twentieth-century writers Mary Antin and Samuel Ornitz
"favored . . . abandonment of Judaism,"[3] Abraham Cahan, Ludwig
30

Lewisohn, and Maurice Samuel championed their religious heritage. It was their attitudes that would transcend the self-hatred of Ben Hecht and Albert Halper and characterize post–World War Two Jewish literature. Following the Holocaust and the creation of Israel, Jewish-American authors have reevaluated their origins and proclaimed the beauty and nobility of Judaic traditions. There have been critics of course. Philip Roth, Bruce Jay Friedman, and Mordecai Richler (a Canadian in the American tradition)[4] come to mind. However their target is not Judaism but the gross materialism of assimilated Jews which is ridiculed in *Good-Bye Columbus, A Mother's Kisses,* and *The Apprenticeship of Duddy Kravitz.* Despite such satire, the authors possess a vision of a different Judaism, a religion and culture which is ethical, dignified, and inspirational. Unlike many of their black counterparts, Jewish writers do not reject religion but wish to reform it.

In modern black literature there are few Chaim Potoks or Charles Angoffs to "defend the faith."[5] Anne Moody's *Coming of Age in Mississippi* does praise Martin Luther King, but at the end she doubts the efficacy of Christian values. Instead, much of twentieth-century Afro-American literature characterizes Christianity as either ineffectual or destructive. In Nella Larsen's *Quicksand* beautiful, talented but desperate Helga Crane marries the Reverend Green, an insensitive, pompous preacher, who drags her into a life of misery. The black church (little distinction is made amongst sects) is condemned as white society's invention to subjugate Negroes. In Ralph Ellison's *Invisible Man* the Reverend Homer Barbee peddles the American dream to gullible Negroes. In urging blacks to adopt the white man's ways, he perpetuates the Horatio Alger myth. Baldwin's *Go Tell it on the Mountain* explicitly identifies black Christianity, its values and rituals, with impotency. The storefront church which shields its congregation from ghetto violence and white hostility demands degrading self-denial and submission.

By contrast, religion strengthens not undermines individuals in Jewish-American literature. In Saul Bellow's *Herzog,* the older members of the immigrant generation compare favorably with their acculturated offspring who disintegrate as they drift from "the Wisdom of their Forefathers."[6] In nine novels and numerous short stories, Charles Angoff pays tribute to the joy and richness of his religious heritage. He praises intellectual and humanitarian traditions, peaceful sabbaths and holidays, and an ancient history which binds his characters to each other and their God.

Such cultural identity is absent from most contemporary Afro-American literature where characters have been ripped from their African heritage, forcibly segregated in America, and subjected to an alien white faith. Increasingly, bitterness is expressed towards the white man and his religion. Three centuries removed from their native past, Afro-American writers are less fortunate than their Jewish counterparts who are close to their ancient heritage. Since rejection of Judaism—a history and culture as well as a religion—constitutes self-denial, most contemporary Jewish authors affirm their genesis. Conversely, many black writers must first reject Christianity and negative stereotypes about Africa before they are free to discover and affirm their origins.

The contrast is evident in Richard Wright's and Bernard Malamud's treatment of religion. While Wright regards Christianity as a negative force, fostering self-hatred and shame and depriving blacks of their cultural inheritance (themes particularly explored in *Black Power* and "Man, God Ain't Like That"), Malamud considers Judaism a positive influence, nurturing ethical conduct and pride in self and community. Wright's black Christianity emphasizes humility, submission, and other worldliness—all of which consign Negroes to living deaths. In *Black Boy, Native Son,* and "The Man Who Lived Underground," autocratic churches, self-serving preachers, and hysterical congregations exude death and darkness. Protagonists like Bigger Thomas and Fred Daniels find little in religion to guide them and much to make them rebel. Conversely, in Malamud's works Judaism's intellectual tradition encourages questioning and self-analysis. Emphasis on earthly welfare and a personal relationship with the God of the Covenant results in constructive social change. Although Malamud's Judaism is primarily personal and noninstitutionalized, wise rabbis, helpful congregations, and meaningful rituals do appear in *The Assistant, The Fixer,* "Angel Levine," "Man in the Drawer," and "Idiots First" among others. For Wright Christianity is associated with the "lake of fire," (*Black Boy,* p. 101), the raging flames of hell. For Malamud Judaism is characterized by the menorah, the ancient symbol of life. Such differences are best illustrated first through an analysis of Wright's ancestral origins in

Africa and Malamud's roots in Eastern Europe. The rest of this chapter will investigate the role of church, preacher, and Christian rituals and values in Wright's fiction; and the function of synagogue, rabbi, and Judaic rituals and values in Malamud's works.

In *Black Power* Wright examined Christianity's destructive impact on Africans and Afro-Americans. Both British imperialists and American slave masters, he believed, used the church to tame "the savages." Unknowingly missionaries contributed to white supremacy with unfortunate consequences for the blacks. Africans were treated as pagan children unable to govern themselves. Their traditions were labelled barbarous; their high priests and medicine men were stripped of authority, and the natives were made dependent on whites. Severe psychological problems developed. Like American Negroes, Africans "lived uneasily and frustratedly in two worlds . . . believing in neither of them" (*Black Power*, p. 37). Although Wright felt alienated in West Africa, a stranger to its languages and customs, he saw in African suffering a reflection of his own and of his people's. "Nothing can give back that pride in themselves, that capacity to make decisions," he wrote. "Today the ruins of their former culture . . . are reflected in timidity, hesitancy and bewilderment" (*Black Power*, p. 153). Wright especially worried about the urban Africans. Geographically and psychologically dislocated, they adjusted poorly to complex city life. Christianity had not fostered discipline, responsibility, and independence, essential traits for survival in the Western society it represented. Nor could urban blacks easily return to the tribe or community whose traditions they were taught to scorn.

Such problems dominate Wright's only African tale, "Man, God Ain't Like That," a parable portraying the corruption of black innocence by designing whites. Trouble is predictable from the moment the arrogant Franklins and their car, representatives of a destructive technological society, intrude on the pristine wilderness and collide with Babu, a black Adam, loyal to his ancestors and tribal customs, but also tempted by the white man and his religion. Instead of criticizing the Franklins for running him over, he apologizes for bloodying their car. Just as he offers animal sacrifices to propitiate his dead father, he sacrifices himself on the altar of white power. Wright further indicts Christianity's effects on the trusting natives by juxtaposing Babu's hymns to Jesus with examples of the Franklins' callousness. A new trinity—Christ, the white man, and the car—

divide the African's loyalties and remove him from his Eden.

Unfortunately, the Franklins are unworthy gods who exploit the faithful. They adopt Babu, but call him an animal, a "baboon, a monkey, . . . an ape" (*Eight Men*, pp. 183, 186)—terms also applied to Bigger Thomas, Tyree Tucker and other characters—and they mock his ancestor worship. By taking him to France, they tantalize him with western wealth, but they are ignorant of his needs and unwilling to share their good life with him. Not surprisingly, Babu, awed by airplanes and skyscrapers, disappears into the concrete jungle and returns three months later, prepared to relinquish his African religion for Christianity which he believes can improve African life. Convinced that Franklin is Jesus, he decides to kill him to be rewarded as whites had been for crucifying Christ. Despite Franklin's protests, Babu cannot be dissuaded; he has been indoctrinated too well. Taught by rote, instructed to accept western mythology unquestioningly, and impressed by white technology, he is confused and embraces Christianity as white magic. Having foresaken his native religion, Babu can no longer return to Africa. Ironically, when he beheads his "Massa," he believes he is being a good Christian. Where earlier he had sacrificed chickens, he now kills a man. In Wright's view Christianity is much more destructive than the pagan faiths it replaced.

Intended as satire, the story is not a subtle exploration of characters' psyches but an attack on Christianity and imperialism for crushing black culture and lives. Even though Babu is an African, he begins to resemble Wright's unhappy Afro-Americans. Simple, naive, and innocent, he becomes dissatisfied and envious when he sees the contrast between black and white living standards. In *Native Son* Bigger, watching the film "Trader Horn," compares naked Africans with carefree "white men and women dressed in [smart] clothes (p. 25). Similarly, Babu, observing "The white man's heaven, . . . [wonders] 'why God give white man buildings and He no give black man same . . . Black man live in jungle. White man live in stone house. Why God do that?' " (p. 186). The question demands an answer that neither Franklin nor the church can give. Wright's message is explicit. Deprive a people of their traditions and self-respect, impose a hollow Christianity, and both blacks and whites will suffer.

In *The Long Dream* Fishbelly Tucker and his friends mock their African heritage. Provoked by Sam, son of a black nationalist, they explode, angry at being reminded of their background. " 'Who [wants to] go to Africa?' Fishbelly asks [his friends] Zeke [and]Tony [who] reply, 'Nobody but damn fools [and] fatheads. Sam wants us to get naked and run wild and eat with our hands and live in mud huts!' " (p. 35). So repugnant is Africa's image that only under pressure will Fish admit to his African ancestry. A similar psychological conflict develops in *Lawd Today* when Jake Jackson and his friends observe a parade by "the International Negro Uplift Association and the African Communities Council" (p. 94). As the proud uniformed black men and women march by with American and African flags, the onlookers feel confused. Their own drooping shoulders, shuffling gaits, and empty lives contrast unfavorably with the marchers' postures. Momentarily they are awed by "the supreme generals of a mythical African republic" (p. 93). However, they quickly reject the Pan-African movement as foolish and crazy. Like Fishbelly and his pals, Jake and his friends refuse association with Africa, a dark, mysterious, threatening place. But they also have doubts about their own debased lives. When a black woman with straightened hair and powdered face emerges from a beauty parlor, her appearance jolts Jake, who "out of the depths of a confused mood, [murmurs] 'maybe them folks is right, who knows?' "(p. 96).

The confusion, however, is never resolved; Wright and his protagonists remain ambivalent about their African heritage. They are, as Sam realizes, neither African nor American. By his own description "a lost son" (*Black Power,* p. 31), the author spent his life searching for traditions, for a community with which he could identify. His quest took him to Africa, but centuries of dispersion, slavery, and humiliation made him uncomfortable in his ancestral homeland. Nor was he able to adjust to Afro-American culture which he viewed as accommodationist and second rate. In the absence of black literary traditions which he could respect,[7] Wright forged his own.

As the father of a militant Afro-American literature,[8] Wright provides a contrast with Bernard Malamud, acclaimed "the most Jewish of American Jewish writers."[9] In the latter's works one hears, as Earl Rovit has commented, "the eternal chant"[10] of Jewish suffering and hope, of centuries of Jewish history. Unlike Wright, Malamud, the son of Eastern European immigrants, grew up with personal knowledge of his heritage, the Torah's ethical principles,

Yiddish folkways and speech, imported from the "shtetl," a self-contained, "highly formalized [Eastern European village] community."[11] Years of persecution and self-imposed restrictions had divorced the "shtetl" from gentile society and created a community at times "provincial, superstitious, and even corrupt,"[12] but also intellectual, disciplined, and idealistic. The "shtetl," a place of despair and hope, both sustained and suffocated its people who "walked around with . . . history on [their] backs."[13] In it Jews felt themselves the Chosen. Insulated from others, they could honor God's 613 commandments, and be rewarded for their "mitzvahs" (good deeds). But they were also victims, a persecuted minority who jokingly described themselves as the people chosen to suffer. Since religious and secular life were finely interwoven in the "shtetl,"[14] it was more than a place; it was an experience, a reenactment of Jewish history with all of its blessings and burdens. As such the "shtetl" has survived the Holocaust and has been used by Malamud and others as a metaphor for Jewish suffering and sacrifice.

Although the "shtetl" as place appears only in *The Fixer,* its impact is felt on Malamud's other works. Many of the immigrants in *The Magic Barrel, Idiots First,* and *The Assistant* transplant the Old World to the New (a development examined in chapter 4.) Therefore, it is important to examine the European setting from which many fled and many later longed for. Unlike Wright's Negroes who are forced to view their origins through the white man's distorted lens, Malamud's Jews have direct experience: either, like Morris Bober and Yakov Bok, they are born in European ghettos, or they encounter Jewish refugees as do Arthur Fidelman, Henry Freeman, and other assimilated American Jews. Such personal contact provides a basis for choosing to accept or reject their background. Bober flees Russian anti-Semitism but carries his Judaism with him; Bok tries to escape both.

In *The Fixer* the "shtetl" is synonymous with Jewishness, which for Malamud is a mixture of pain and joy. Like its culture, the "shtetl" is ancient, crowded, and changeless. Bok, seeking new ideas, opportunities, and experiences, finds the ghetto oppressive. But as Shmuel, his father-in-law, reminds him, " 'the world is in the shtetl—people, their trials, worries [and] circumstances' "(*The Fixer,* p. 12). On weekdays the market is filled with Jews trading goods, swapping gossip, and exchanging confidences. On Friday evenings the soft glow of candles brightens the countryside. The Sabbath is peaceful. Of course Bok remembers how fragile such peace is, how Cossacks can desecrate the holidays and holy people by plundering, slaughtering, and stuffing "white sausage into [the] mouth [of] . . . a black-bearded Jew" (p. 5). He recalls his own parents who remained in the "shtetl," their sanctuary, and were murdered there. He tries to escape the burden of being Jewish, but it is not easy. Even after he cuts his hair, shaves his beard, discards his prayer things, and visits a church, Bok is still a Jew to himself and others. "For a Jew," he realizes, "it was the same wherever he went; he carried a remembered pack on his back" (p. 315). He had exchanged the "shtetl's" offer of friendship, occasional work, and traditional food—"a hardboiled egg with a pinch of salt . . . [and] sour cream with cut-up potato" (p. 213)—for a Russian dungeon. That was a poor trade. Worse, "he hadn't identified himself as a Jew by birth." He had sold his birthright for material rewards and had increased his "self-contempt" (p. 41). Unlike Wright's Negroes who feel shame because of their African heritage, Bok feels shame for denying his origins. His mistake costs him his freedom and teaches him that "the more one hides the more one has to" (p. 41).

The lesson is repeated in "Lady of the Lake," "The Last Mohican," and "Man in the Drawer," stories of Jewish-American self-discovery abroad. In all three tales American Jews indifferent or hostile to their origins seek fulfillment in Europe, scene of the Holocaust. Instead, they encounter European Jews who make ethnic amnesia impossible. In "Lady of the Lake," Henry Levin, a Jewish malcontent, calls himself Henry R. Freeman in an attempt to reject "the past [and] . . . the limitations it had imposed on him" (*The Magic Barrel*, p. 105). In search of romance and adventure, he falls in love with Isabella del Dongo whose classic beauty, he believes, reflects a proud, noble Italian ancestry far superior to the Jewish heritage he conceals. Ironically, however, the history he admires is his own, for Isabella, a lower-class Italian Jew, is also an imposter. Both frauds, the two appear well-matched, but their deception differs in degree and purpose. Isabella's lies are short-lived, designed to keep Freeman on the island until she can determine if he is Jewish and thereby eligible to become her husband. She quickly reveals her economic status and repeatedly hints about her religion. Only Freeman's obtuseness and anti-Semitism make him misinterpret her references to Judaism. While Isabella temporarily conceals her heritage, she never considers forsaking it. On the other hand, Freeman, one of Malamud's few self-hating Jews, resembles Wright's characters except that he is contemptible, while they are pitiable. Enslaved, persecuted, and deprived of their culture, they are forced to accept the white man's image of a savage Africa. Conversely, Levin-Freeman chooses freely to reject Judaism because it has inconvenienced him. Unlike the oppressed Bok who regrets his treachery, Freeman has no qualms about repudiating his people by "forget[ting] that he had been born Jewish . . . and marry[ing] . . . in a church" ("Lady of the Lake," p. 126). But his betrayal of the Covenant costs him Isabella who reveals the concentration camp numbers on her breast and declares that she can't marry a gentile because her " 'past is meaningful to [her. She] treasure[s] what [she] suffered for' " (p. 132). By denying his past, Freeman is denied a future; Isabella flees, leaving him to "embrace only moonlit stone" (p. 133) symbolizing the cold, hard empty life awaiting him.

A similar scene occurs at the end of "The Last Mohican" when Arthur Fidelman attempts to make amends to the refugee Susskind and is left beseeching empty air. In Italy to study Giotto, Fidelman is more interested in Roman history than his own. The catacombs, convents, and churches are more important than the Jewish quarter with its synagogue and cemetery. But Susskind, an Eastern European "schnorrer" (beggar) changes Fidelman. His " 'Shalom' "[15] compels the art student to return the greeting and reluctantly admit his Jewishness. "An obnoxious immigrant,"[16] he angers Fidelman by demanding money and clothes and later stealing part of his manuscript. But he also awakens the latter to the importance of charity, compassion, and ethnic loyalty. While searching for his missing chapter and its thief, Fidelman is led from romantic Rome to "the horrors of Jewish history, past and present."[17] In the cold, unheated synagogue, in the crowded, decaying, ancient ghetto, and in the neglected cemetery, burial site of Nazi victims, Fidelman confronts his past and becomes a Jew. Asked by the synagogue's beadle if he is Susskind's relative, he replies " 'not exactly' " (p. 174), which is a partial admission of his ties with the refugee and all Jews. Where earlier he had avoided Yiddish, he now uses some when he speaks to Susskind. A visit to the refugee's room, "a pitch black freezing cave" (p. 186) moves him to offer his coveted suit to Susskind who reveals that he has destroyed the worthless chapter. Temporarily reverting to his old self, Fidelman angrily chases the refugee through the Jewish quarter until he recognizes his error, but unfortunately it is too late. Harried by history, Susskind races from his latest tormentor, who like Henry Freeman, is unable to expiate his sin. However, like Bok, both men learn that "the more one hides, the more one has to" (*The Fixer*, p. 41).

Wherever Malamud's Jews travel, they are reminded of their ethnic roots. In "Man in the Drawer" Howard Harvitz, another American Jew, tours the Soviet Union to forget his problems and gather material for magazine articles. Instead he encounters Feliks Levitansky, a Russian Susskind, who utters " 'Shalom' " and appeals for help in getting his manuscripts published (*Rembrandt's Hat*, p. 34). Although the setting is contemporary U.S.S.R., it is interchangeable with tzarist Russia. Seventy years after the Beiliss-Bok case, little has changed. Soviet secret police have replaced tzarist inquisitors; Levitansky calls himself an atheist instead of a freethinker, but these differences are superficial. The mood is still furtive, the atmosphere dangerous as the men, separated by citizenship and language, hesitatingly recognize each other. Richard Wright felt estranged from West Africans, but Malamud's Harvitz and Levitansky are drawn together. What, one wonders, binds the two strangers "from the moment [they] meet" (p. 34)? Their political convictions are a source of friction. Neither are religious Jews. Their writing provides a basis for a relationship, but it is not enough to explain their attachment to each other. The explanation is rooted in history. Beyond linguistic, national, and political differences, they share a common heritage, based not on ritual or belief in God, but on a loyalty to Jews and their history. The bond, a mystical and indefinable one, compels Levitansky to risk his career and freedom by writing about Jews. It moves a frightened and reluctant Harvitz to smuggle the Russian's manuscripts into America. It is a bond admired by Frederick Douglass and Booker T. Washington who urged American Negroes to imitate Jewish unity.[18]

In this story, as in *The Fixer*, "The Last Mohican," and others, Malamud defines Jewishness as a willingness to honor the Covenant by sacrificing and suffering for freedom and justice. A good Jew assumes responsibility for all the needy, but has a special obligation to his people. A good Jew awakens others to iniquities. Thus Shmuel,

Susskind, and Levitansky prod Bok, Fidelman, and Harvitz to fulfill their moral duties. In addition, Jews must be familiar with their history, proud of their identity, and prepared to maintain it under any circumstances. In this sense Harvitz and Levitansky are similar. Both "marginal Jews" (*Rembrandt's Hat,* p. 37), they nevertheless are attracted to Jewish culture. Despite Levitansky's insistence that he is a Soviet nationalist only writing incidentally about Jews, his stories reveal, as Harvitz observes, " 'a strong sympathy for Jews' " (p. 61). Both men visit synagogues; the former to gather material for his stories; the latter " 'to be refreshed by the language and images of a time and place where God was' " (p. 60). Moreover, both retain their Jewish names. Out of respect for his gentile mother's wishes, Levitansky honors his father by keeping his name.[19] Similarly, Harvitz chooses to " 'be closer to [his] true self' " (p. 37) by reclaiming the family name which his father, a practical minded doctor, had changed to Harris. Ironically, while many of Malamud's European Jews take great risks to preserve their heritage, some American Jews eagerly shed theirs. Unlike Wright's characters, however, they are pursued by their past and given a chance to recover their identity.

For Malamud, Judaism is a way of life and a history transcending national boundaries and transmitted from generation to generation. Organized, institutionalized religion is not important in his fiction. Although rabbis, synagogues, and rituals are depicted, they are subordinate to the individual who is personally responsible for maintaining the Covenant. According to legend, God selected the Jews to uphold His Law but they also agreed to do His bidding. No messiah can intervene on their behalf; no clergy can absolve them of wrongdoings. Nor should promise of rewards or punishments in the next world motivate ethical conduct in this one. Malamud's Jews (and non-Jews, products of the same vision) are expected to be good because it is the right way to live. " 'My father used to say to be a Jew all you need is a good heart' " (*The Assistant,* p. 124), Morris Bober tells Frank Alpine. The Law, he believes, allows men to distinguish between good and evil. It separates man from animal. Repeatedly freedom of choice is emphasized and the protagonists' better natures are appealed to. " 'You'll invent your way out . . . if you only keep trying,' " Olga, a lonely middle-aged woman, advises Mitka about his writing and his life ("The Girl of My Dreams," p. 39). " 'I suffer for you. . . . You suffer for me' " (*The Assistant*, p. 125), Morris expresses his faith in his assistant's humanity. " 'You are responsible . . . as a man [and] . . . a Jew' " (*Pictures of Fidelman*, p. 16), Susskind informs Fidelman. Such scenes often appear in Malamud's fiction, but they are always part of long exchanges as the protagonists question and probe, trying to discover why they should be good men and responsible for others. Ultimately they are guided by their consciences but they have had the benefit of moral tutors who prod them to consider their purpose in life and who appeal to their sense of decency.

Wright and his protagonists are not so fortunate. Instead of helpful guidance, they receive rigid indoctrination. In the autobiographical *Black Boy*, the author identifies Negro religion with white repression. Both foster unwarranted shame and guilt. Church emphasis on original sin reinforces guilt about skin color. In both cases the Negro is marked from birth and made to feel guilty over that which he cannot control. Whites equate black with evil; the church stresses man's innate wickedness. Together they convince Negroes of their inferiority. Understandably, then, Wright depicts his grandmother as the most oppressive, powerful figure in the family. Nearly white and fanatically religious, she represents the conspiracy of white society and black church to restrain Negroes. Rigid, humorless, and harshly disciplinarian, Granny struggles to prove her purity, her whiteness by cleansing the sinners around her. Unlike Morris Bober who quietly illustrates the importance of virtue, Granny rants about vice. The one identifies Jewishness with goodness; the other associates blackness with wickedness. Richard is subjected to unending sermons about his black soul. The smallest infraction indicates that he is a "Black devil" (*Black Boy*, p. 37). Cleanliness of soul, mind, and body are stressed constantly. But baths and prayers cannot change reality: Richard is black; his mother and brother are black; and Granny with her few drops of Negro blood is black. Ultimately they have to face the fact that white society and the black church make salvation possible only in the next life. Some, especially Wright's women, accept such precepts and redouble their efforts to gain entry into heaven. Others, particularly his young male protagonists, remain skeptical about a religion which values death more than life. They require answers but receive lectures or sermons. Abrupt exclamations and loud declarations stifle any questions. " 'Don't say that,' "Wright is warned.

" 'God may never forgive you' " (*Black Boy*, p. 127). Don't do that, he is told, or " 'you're going to burn in hell' " (p. 48). Such religious attitudes stiffen Wright's resistance to the church.

The clergy reinforce Wright's contempt for religion. In *Black Religion* Joseph Washington observes that many black preachers "succumbed to the cajolery and bribery of the white power structure and became its foil. Instead of freedom [they] preached moralities and emphasized rewards in the life beyond. They increased [their] control and [manipulated] the folk . . . for purposes of gaining personal power."[20] With the exception of the Reverend Taylor in "Fire and Cloud," Wright's ministers resemble Washington's portrait. The list of self-serving and ineffectual preachers is long. In *Black Boy* the local minister who gluttonously consumes Mrs. Wright's food, boorishly dominates the conversation, and laughs at young Richard's protests reminds the author of his insensitive father who "was used to having his own way" (p. 23). Many of Wright's preachers are more interested in their own well-being than in the welfare of poor blacks. Timid and fearful of white authorities, they urge their flock to trust in God and seek salvation in the next world.

In *The Long Dream* the Reverend Ragland, whose name suggests shabbiness, avoids reality by rationalizing untimely Negro deaths as God's will. At a mass funeral service for forty-three fire victims and for Tyree Tucker, victim of a white man's bullet, the reverend refuses to blame whites who, he says, are only God's instruments. In the tradition of the Reverends Green, Homer Barbee, and Gabriel Grimes, Ragland encourages passivity and obedience. The relationship between Ragland and his pitiful congregation parallels that of whites and blacks. As God's self-appointed spokesman, he commands and chastises the faithful who echo his praise of death and the afterlife. Some of those who died, he argues, were sinners, called to account before God. Others were the virtuous, summoned to enjoy the kingdom of heaven. Thus, whites are freed of any responsibility and Negroes discouraged from questioning their fate.

In *Native Son* a similar philosophy guides the "well-dressed" Reverend Hammond who stretches forth a "dingy palm" (p. 240) to comfort Bigger Thomas on trial for murder. In an interminable, droning sermon, he urges the sinner to welcome death. " 'This worl' ain our home. Life ever'day is a crucifixion. . . . Be like Jesus. Don't resist' " (p. 243). Throughout the prison scene Wright's revulsion is barely concealed. Hammond is brave before defeated black folk like Bigger and his family, but he cowers before whites. When Jan Erlone, the murdered girl's Communist boyfriend, enters the cell, Hammond takes "a step backward [and] bow[s]" (p. 243). But once he realizes the Communists want to defend Bigger, he speaks up. "In a tone that [is] militant, but deferring" (p. 246), Hammond urges that Bigger's fate be left in God's hands. The Communists want to save Bigger to further their own interests. The Reverend appears willing to sacrifice him to avoid antagonizing whites. Both treat Bigger as an object.

The Outsider, written years later, explicitly identifies communism as a new white religion, intent on dominating blacks. Party cells replace churches; Communist officials rule instead of ministers; Negroes are sacrificed for the greater good. " 'Know why I don't go to church?' " Sarah protests to her husband, a loyal Communist worker, " 'Cause I have to *kneel* in front of that white priest. . . . Now, we're in the revolution and the *same* goddamn white man comes along. But he's in the Party now' " (*The Outsider,* p. 176). Of course Sarah can kneel in front of a black priest but according to Wright she still would be worshipping white power. This view also appears in "Fire and Cloud" which sympathetically depicts the problems of a black preacher who is pressured by Southern authorities, Communist officials, and his own congregation. Clearly the most admirable of Wright's clergymen, the Reverend Taylor (discussed in chapter 1) risks his position and possibly his life to lead starving blacks and whites in a successful demonstration for food. But his defiance of white authorities does not prove his independence, for the march is Communist inspired and planned. Although one of the party members is black, a white exerts the most pressure on Taylor. Intended as a tribute to interracial cooperation and to communism, the story also reveals black dependency on an ideology conceived by whites. Taylor does emerge as a triumphant black leader, but he is also used by the Communists. Even so, he is a rarity in Wright's fiction. Given the origins of black Christianity and the history of American Negroes, it is not surprising that most of the author's clergy are rigid men who preach resignation and other-worldly salvation. The fact that most of Wright's works predate the contemporary civil rights movement also explains the absence of strong black ministers in his fiction.

The opposite occurs in Malamud's fiction which is characterized by an absence of religious conformity and hierarchy. The author's liberal Judaism encompasses characters of varied backgrounds and convictions. " 'A wonderful thing,' Manischevitz says [in "Angel Levine"]. There are Jews everywhere' " (*The Magic Barrel,* p. 56). And of course he is right. Black, Italian, German, Russian, and American Jews appear in Malamud's works. Theologically they include the orthodox Shmuel, the ethical but nonobservant Morris Bober, and the convert Frank Alpine. Obviously no doctrinaire clergy can claim the loyalty of such a group. Nor do any attempt to do so. The few rabbis who appear in Malamud's fiction emphasize compassion, justice, and earthly well-being. Except for two Russian rabbis, the others are free from the external political and social pressures which shape Wright's preachers. Consequently, they represent a flexible, tolerant Judaism concerned with individual freedom and worth. At Morris Bober's funeral, for example, the rabbi pays tribute to the grocer, a " 'true Jew because he lived in the Jewish experience, which he remembered, and with a Jewish heart.' " Although he doesn't " 'excuse' " Morris for violating Judaism's " 'formal tradition,' " he praises him for being " 'true to the spirit of [Jewish] life—to want for others that which he wants also for himself. . . . He suffered, he endured, but with hope' " (*The Assistant,* p. 229). The contrast between the Reverand Ragland's funeral oration and the rabbi's eulogy is striking. The former belittles the dead person and recounts his sins; the latter praises him and emphasizes his virtues. The one glorifies death; the other affirms life.

For Malamud's rabbis the spirit is more important than the letter of the Law, as Leo Finkle, a rabbinical student in "The Magic Barrel," realizes. Leo is the antithesis of most of Wright's preachers. True, he is an egotist and a perfectionist, demanding that the marriage broker provide him with the perfect wife. But he is also honest with himself and others. He refuses to allow Salzman to describe him as a great rabbi. More importantly, his conscience forces him to admit that he has entered the rabbinate because he feels "unloved and loveless." Familiar with Judaic Law, Finkle understands "that he [does] not love God as well as he might, because he ha[s] not loved man" (*The Magic Barrel,* p. 205). It is inconceivable that most of Wright's sanctimonious ministers could make such an admission or consider sacrificing their positions in order to become true Christians. Ragland and Hammond are too self-satisfied and righteous even to question their own conduct. On the other hand, Finkle has the makings of a good rabbi, one who remains a life-long student, willing to examine his motives and learn from others. But faith and insight are not enough. Once aware of his inadequacy, he must act. By jeopardizing his career to help Stella, Salzman's "wild" daughter, he can become a good Jew and a rabbi true to the spirit of Judaism. Finkle's glory, like the prophet Hosea's (Hos. 1:2), rests in "converting [a prostitute] to goodness" and thus converting "himself to God" (p. 213). By offering himself to Stella, Finkle, like all of Malamud's good Jews, accepts the Covenant, the "Yoke of the Law,"[21] the burdens in return for the blessings and happiness he hopes to receive in this life.

Similar clerical compassion is displayed in "Idiots First" when a poor, sickly rabbi ignores his wife's protests and relinquishes his only valuable possession in order to save a life. Unlike the gluttonous preacher in *Black Boy* who mocks young Richard's hunger, the rabbi sacrifices his fur-lined caftan to enable a dying Jew to provide for his retarded son. The motto "Tsdokeh [charity] will save from death"[22] governs behavior in "Idiots First" and in most of Malamud's fiction. But it is anti-Semitic Russia which most strongly tests rabbinical courage and selflessness. In "Man in the Drawer" two frightened rabbis are torn between loyalty to their conscience and obedience to the Soviet government. Approached by an old Jew seeking matzohs for Passover, the first rabbi hesitates to help because matzoh distribution is illegal. Ultimately, however, he relents and is faithful to his tradition which emphasizes charity and Jewish interdependence. The scene recalls Yakov Bok's risking his freedom by sheltering an old Chassid on Passover. In both cases the matzoh is simultaneously the unleavened "staff of life" and the potential instrument of death. To exalt life, chances are taken with death. Malamud's clergy, however, are not always brave. The second rabbi in "Man in the Drawer" resembles the Reverends Ragland and Hammond. Afraid that a young man illegally selling a prayer shawl can endanger himself and the congregation, the rabbi begs him to leave. However, unlike Ragland, the rabbi does not justify his cowardice by shifting responsibility to God.

In the collection of short stories, *Rembrandt's Hat*, a more complex portrait of a rabbi emerges in "The Silver Crown" which focuses on the relationship between Albert Gans, a cynical Jew, and Rabbi Jonas Lifschitz, a faith-healer who tries to help him. Part charlatan, part compassionate teacher, Lifschitz demands $986 to craft a silver crown (a memorial to God, Zech. 6:14) which will heal Albert's dying father. Slimy, unkempt, and shifty like Susskind and Salzman, the rabbi arouses Albert's suspicions. His questionable ritual, his insistence on cash, and his unwillingess to reveal the crown create an image of a faker. Another rabbi's intimation that Lifschitz is now rich enough to attend a palatial synagogue only adds to the impression. Thus, when Albert, a stingy high school teacher, discovers Lifschitz and his deformed daughter strolling in expensive clothing, he is outraged and tries to recover his money.

But as usual in Malamud's fiction appearances are deceptive. Certainly Lifschitz has used the money for himself, but that is besides the point. Faithful to his calling and his name (Lifschitz means protector of life in Yiddish), the rabbi tries to teach the teacher that charity, faith, and love are inseparable. Though he profits from the transaction, he performs a useful service by showing Albert a mirror in which a menorah, the dying father, the rabbi, and the silver crown (symbols of life, compassion, faith, and charity) all appear. Temporarily awed, Albert grudgingly pays the rabbi, but once the vision vanishes, his skepticism returns. Like the miser in an old traditional Chassidic tale, he "shuts [himself] off from his fellow men and from humanity itself"[23] by refusing to recognize that life cannot be measured in dollars. Lifschitz holds a mirror up to him, but he refuses to see that he must love, honor, and sacrifice for his father. The son sees only himself, and thus his father dies from a broken heart. Still the fault is not the rabbi's. He can guide and inspire, but it is up to the individual to become a "mensch" (humane individual). Unlike most of Wright's preachers, Malamud's rabbis believe that no amount of exhortation or coercion can change character.

The absence of religious conformity is also reflected in the places and manner of worship in Malamud's fiction. The Jewish temple is a grimy room in "The Mourners," a jail cell in *The Fixer,* and a graveyard in *The Assistant.* Since prayer, the individual's communication with his conscience and God, can take place anywhere, Malamud's few synagogue services vary from each other. In "Angel Levine," the house of worship, a former Harlem tavern, contains four black Jews engaged in a Talmudic debate. In "The Last Mohican" organ music wafts through a cathedral-like synagogue where Italian Jews are praying. In "The Silver Crown" a storefront houses a rabbi and his poor congregation of a dozen Jews. With such variety, one is tempted to echo Manischevitz's " 'There are Jews everywhere.' " Despite such external differences, however, all the synagogues serve a similar function: they help Malamud's misguided protagonists who stumble into them. For example, Manischevitz, a troubled Job-like figure, searching for the black angel Levine, finds himself alone and frightened in Harlem, until he chances upon a group of four black Jews analyzing the Torah. "Touched by this sight from his childhood and youth, Manischevitz enters" (p. 53), listens to the exchange about the meaning of "neshoma" (soul), which exists in all men, and is told where to find Levine. The incident persuades Manischevitz that Levine may be a black Jew as he has claimed. Fortified and less skeptical, he can express faith in the black angel's power to save him.

In "The Last Mohican" the synagogue in which Fidelman searches for Susskind has marble floors, holy water, and organ music. The atmosphere seems to be a strange blend of Catholic and Jewish symbols until the beadle approaches Fidelman and in a Jewish accent asks where he is from. Responding to questions about Susskind, the beadle urges him to search the ghetto again. The advice is significant, for although Fidelman does not find the refugee there, he discovers his own Jewish past which changes his feelings about Susskind. A similar quest is undertaken in "The Silver Crown" when an angry Albert searches a storefront synagogue for Lifschitz. Unlike Manischevitz, the teacher, a stranger to Judaic values and ritual, feels uncomfortable in the "shul" (synagogue). Nevertheless, before he leaves, one worshipper gently touches him and invites him to stay. To Albert's reply that he is "looking for a friend," the man says, " 'look, maybe you'll find him' " (*Rembrandt's Hat*, p. 25). Unfortunately the teacher's selfishness and bitterness make him less able than Manischevitz or Fidelman to accept such guidance.

In all three stories synagogues serve as beacons of light to wandering Jews in need of direction. By contrast, the atmosphere in Wright's churches is claustrophobic and death-like. For Wright and other black writers most Negro churches were indifferent to life. In *Black Boy* "terrifyingly sweet hymns" (p. 168), joyous outbursts, and powerful sermons praise death which will free suffering Negroes from this world. The faithful will be rewarded in heaven, but darkness, fire, and brimstone await nonbelievers like Wright. Repent, come forth, be baptized, for "this may be the last" chance (p. 168), he is warned. Only God's holy water can purify the sinner and save him from the "lake of fire" (p. 128). Pressured by the preacher, urged by his friends, and beseeched by his tearful mother, Wright allows himself to be "saved." But the ritual has the opposite effect. The baptismal water "rolling down [his] neck and . . . back [feels] like insects crawling" (p. 171). He feels dirtied, not cleansed for having betrayed his conscience.

Years later Wright re-created his religious experience in his fiction. The hot, close, suffocating church, the symbols of fire and water, of Christ writhing on the Cross spell death and damnation to his black protagonists. In *The Long Dream* the Reverend Ragland delivers a "stomping" dramatic funeral oration in a "stifling hot" (p. 320) church, filled with five thousand perspiring bodies and forty-three corpses. Blended with the "cloying sweetness" (p. 320) of floral wreaths, the stench of sweat and death nauseates Fishbelly as he hears the theatrical reverend and the hysterical congregation welcome God's judgment on Tyree Tucker. Like Wright, Fish condemns the church's necrophilia. Filled with burnt bodies and a suffering congregation, the church symbolizes physical and spiritual death. The holy lake of fire, the flames of hell are not in the next world but in this one. They are not merely symbols but reality both within the church and without.

Wright associates the charred flesh in the Reverend Ragland's church with the mutilated body of Bobo, a black youth burned alive by whites in "Big Boy Leaves Home." In "Fire and Cloud" "a ring of fire" (*Uncle Tom's Children*, p. 163) encircles the Reverend Taylor as he is whipped and forced on bended knees to say the Lord's Prayer, emphasizing his humility and submission to God's will. A white mob's fiery cross greets Bigger Thomas when he is returned to the scene of his crime. Even working in a church can result in death as Saul Saunders discovers in "The Man Who Killed A Shadow." A janitor "in the National Cathedral [he enjoys his] solitary kind of work" (*Eight Men*, p. 198) until the white church librarian provokes him to murder. Religion literally relegates Wright's protagonists to the netherworld as Fred Daniels realizes in "The Man Who Lived Underground." Partially influenced by The Book of Daniel, the allegorical tale depicts the protagonist's desperate attempt to pierce illusion and reveal truth. Drawn by the sound of hymns, he spies through a sewer crevice on a basement church which contains a dark, funereal room with "black men and women dressed in white robes, singing, holding tattered songbooks in the black palms" (*Eight Men*, p. 32). Unable to reconcile the stench and poverty with hymns of love and joy, Daniels is repelled by the spectacle of "black people grovelling and begging for [heavenly salvation]" (p. 33). Still he recognizes that their illusions merely reflect white indoctrination. By juxtaposing the poor black church with the money, jewels, and guns which Daniels finds in adjacent white establishments, Wright comments on the economic and political disparity between blacks and whites. But he also illustrates the spiritual bankruptcy of both black religion and white society which worship foolish goals and false gods. Like the prophet Daniel who warned Belshazzar against venerating idols (Dan. 6:23), Fred Daniels's judgment is also accurate, but unlike the former, the black prophet is abused and his counsel ignored. The confrontation in the church is highly ironical, for the black congregants label him a dirty, smelly "nigger" but are oblivious to their own stench. Blind to the filth around them, some continue to sing of "sweet Jesus" while others brutally eject Daniels, threatening to throw him to the lions by calling the police.

Clearly, Wright's myopic church, unlike Malamud's synagogue, cannot guide the lost. Its promise of salvation is empty; its baptismal water is dirty, and incapable of purifying desperate black men. In fact, water, like fire, is used as a symbol of death by Wright. In one surrealistic scene Daniels, trying to cleanse himself physically and spiritually, imagines the faucet water turning into blood. In another scene he dreams of himself as Christ walking on water and attempting to save a drowning woman and baby. But Daniels (and by extension Christianity) fails: the sea turns rough, pulling all three into its swirling depths. The sequence foreshadows Daniels's actual death. Rejected by the church, he surrenders to the police who shoot him as he leads them to his hideaway. The last image is one of Daniels's swallowing "thick, bitter water" (p. 92) which becomes his soggy grave. In "Big Boy Leaves Home" the protagonist and his friends invade a white man's swimming hole, but the cooling water turns into a river of hot blood when whites arrive. A variation on this theme appears in *Native Son*. Having successfully held off the police, Bigger becomes the target of their hoses and is overwhelmed by rushing streams of freezing water. Later in prison, when he recalls the icy water, Bigger is visited by the Reverend Hammond who preaches to him about Christ's mercy and prays that the "Lawd [will] wash [his sins] as white snow" (p. 241). The scene underscores the church's delusions, and the inappropriateness of white Christianity's symbols and rituals for suffering Negroes.

Understandably then, most of Wright's protagonists, like their author, reject the church. They are unable to reconcile Christ's saintly crucifix with the K.K.K.'s fiery cross. To embrace the former, as their submissive mothers do, may prolong their lives, but they rebel and are unwilling to pay the price—emasculation and death of the spirit. Like Wright, they "cannot feel weak and lost in a cosmic manner . . . [and they are revolted by how] His creatures serve Him" (*Black Boy*, p. 127). Grovelling before whites is reprehensible but may be necessary; grovelling before God is contemptible. Furthermore, they cannot believe in their mothers' insatiable God who demands complete obedience and sacrifice of all earthly pleasures. Such a God, Wright believed, worsened the Negroes' plight, depriving them of dignity and initiative. Such a God turned sons against mothers. Wright successfully "fought to keep from being crushed" (*Black Boy*, p. 119) by his grandmother's and mother's beliefs.

The struggle, however, left its mark, as is evident in his fiction. In *Native Son* Mrs. Thomas's docility disgusts Bigger who is driven to deny her religion in order to feel manly. When she visits him in prison and begs him to pray for their heavenly reunion, Bigger is nauseated but like Wright, he relents, not wanting to hurt his mother's feelings. With arms locked and heads bowed, they pray, exhibiting "their weakness . . . [and] shame in the presence of [white] powers" (p. 255). The humiliating ritual makes Bigger hate himself and his family. *The Outsider* also illustrates the danger of such religious convictions. Deserted by her husband, Mrs. Damon, like most of Wright's older women, clings to the church and tries to impose her beliefs on her son. But her constant tirades against drinking, gambling, and sex have the opposite effect. To escape emasculation, he rejects both his mother and her faith. Named for the Crucifix, Cross perverts the symbol and instead of suffering for others makes others suffer for him. He hates his mother's God whom he imagines as "an awful face shaped in the form of a huge and crushing NO" (p. 16). This is the God whom Mrs. Tucker worships and Fishbelly denies in *The Long Dream*. " 'It ain't Gawd I feel; it's the white man' " (p. 239). Fish is tempted to scream at his mother. The identification of God and white power appears in *Lawd Today* where religion is a source of friction between husband and wife. Glancing at his wife's religious booklets, Jake Jackson sees a "picture of a haloed, bearded man draped in white folds; the man's hand was resting upon the blond curls of a blue-eyed girl. . . . 'What makes Lil keep all this trash?' [Jake wonders as] he hurl[s] the book across the room" (p. 11). Later he and his friends jokingly discuss the possibility of "Gawd" returning as a "nigger" since He had already appeared as a "Jew" (p. 70). The conversation highlights the different ways Wright and Malamud treat religion.

Wright's protagonists view God as an alien, repressive force; Malamud's perceive Him as a partner in a special relationship. A good Jew who honors the Covenant will expect to be blessed by God. If he is not, he may first examine his own conduct and finding himself blameless, then complain to Him. While Wright's faithful passively accept God's will, most of Malamud's Jews respectfully challenge it. An agreement has been made and God is expected to listen and assist His people in fulfilling their obligations to enrich and preserve life. Thus, in "Angel Levine" Manischevitz, plagued by misfortunes, rails against the Almighty and threatens to become a nonbeliever. The story illustrates "the mutual welfare pact which [supposedly] binds God and the Jews."[24] Once the tailor proves his faith by accepting a Negro angel as God's messenger, he is rewarded by having his wife's health restored. Significantly, in Malamud's fiction miracles occur, and God occasionally intervenes to strengthen the family. In "Idiots First" Mendel, a dying Jew, successfully bargains with death, God's agent, to spare his retarded son. A good man and a devoted father, Mendel demands mercy. Unwilling to accept death passively, he literally battles him, saves his son and reminds God of his obligation to His people.

Not all of Malamud's fiction, however, contains such miracles. At times it appears as though God had turned away from the Jews. The result of such heavenly indifference, however, is earthly skepticism. Thus, in *The Fixer* Yakov Bok alternately blames or doubts God, but unlike Wright's rebels, he does not fear him, and he is willing to admit his own responsibility for his troubles. One passage vividly describes Bok's attitudes towards God and the Jews. Reading the Old Testament, he is "gripped by the narrative of the joyous Hebrews doing business, fighting wars, sinning and worshipping—whatever they were doing always engaged in talk with the huffing-puffing God who tried to sound, maybe out of envy, like a human being. . . . God envies the Jews: it's a rich life" (p. 197). While times have certainly changed in the nineteenth century ghetto, these Jews are descendants of a proud people who used to feel God's presence. Perhaps they and Bok himself have sinned too much. Perhaps, as Shmuel (his orthodox father-in-law) concedes, neither " 'God nor his people are perfect' " (p. 20). Perhaps God can no longer keep up with the Jews. Perhaps God was invented by the Jews. In any case Yahweh is not the "oppressive NO face" described by Cross Damon. Instead of expressing awe or terror of God, Bok feels pity and disappointment. " 'If God's not a man [then] he has to be,' " the fixer decides. Whether or not divinely inspired, the Covenant is worth preserving. Its Law celebrates life and inspires Bok to fight for earthly justice. Ironically, the cynic—the apostate—becomes "the defender of the faith" and renews the several thousand year old agreement. By the novel's end a miracle has occurred: the human spirit has withstood unbelievable degradation and emerged stronger. In the tradition of the "dignified Chassid" whom he had earlier sheltered, Bok commits himself to freedom. Just as the Chassid had commemorated Passover, the exodus of Jews from Bondage, so the fixer will lead a new exodus from Russian slavery.

In their search for the promised land, where decency and liberty flourish, Malamud's characters are guided by religious symbols and rituals. Water, for example, can cleanse and redeem them. Thus, when Fidelman finally sacrifices for love, the Venetian waters turn clean and calm. In a final act of consecration, the artist "dip[s] . . . his hands" (*Pictures of Fidelman*, p. 208) into the sparkling water of his beautifully crafted clear bowl. Later he weeps and kisses Beppo, who has taught him love. The ritual's religious significance becomes apparent in *The Fixer* when the old Chassid "dips his fingers into water" (p. 66), prays to God and then kisses the phylactery, containing the Almighty's words. Both ceremonies are expressions of love, one for man, the other for God. In both rituals water sanctifies as it never does in Wright's fiction. Early in *The Assistant* a simple act reveals Frank Alpine's capacity for goodness and foreshadows his relationship with Morris Bober. Having participated in the robbery, Alpine feels pity for the frightened, wounded grocer and offers him a drink of water. The gesture has religious importance. It partially cleanses and redeems Frank, binding him to the old man whom he tries to help even while he betrays him.

Similarly, prayer, which blinds Wright's Negroes to reality, moves Malamud's Jews to noble action. Kaddish, a solemn hymn of mourning, is not simply an expression of despair. It commemorates, blesses, and unites the dead with the living Jewish community. Thus, at the end of "The Magic Barrel," Salzman's Kaddish blesses Finkle's attempt to reclaim the wayward Stella, pronounced dead by her father. In "The Mourners" the prayer for the dead inspires the living as Kessler, a selfish recluse, and Gruber, his stingy landlord, wrap themselves in white sheets and repent. In "Man in the Drawer" prayer protects, redeems, and unites Jews in the Soviet Union. A Jewish atheist, betrayed to the police for selling a prayer shawl, "drapes [it] over his head and prays [so] passionate a Kaddish . . . that the police hesitate to approach him and the congregants are moved" (p. 91) to join him. The last image, one of a "white shawl luminously praying" (p. 91), suggests a union of the youth with his heritage and transcendence of the latter over the police state.

Realistically, the victory may be temporary. The atheist, in fact the whole congregation, may be carted off to suffer Yakov Bok's fate, but even then, as *The Fixer* indicates, Israel may survive. Where in Wright's fiction is there a comparable vision of religion nurturing pride, justice, and freedom? The courageous Reverend Taylor, of course, comes to mind. But he is clearly an exception among Wright's faithful. Furthermore, Taylor's success depends on cooperating with the Communists and forgetting his Christian humility. Generally Wright's rebels defend themselves by repudiating the church, its values and symbols. Thus, a defeated Bigger Thomas, wearing Reverend Hammond's crucifix, feels betrayed by the sight of the K.K.K.'s flaming cross. Suddenly the preacher's cross was "bloody, not flaming; meek not militant" (*Native Son,* p. 286). Refusing society's burdens, he rips the cross from his throat, and dashing it to the ground, discards the white man's religion and his mother's illusions. The guards are horrified: " 'That's your cross!' " (p. 287) they exclaim. But Bigger knows better. He rejects the role they have chosen for him and substitutes his own nihilistic values. In a conversation with Max, he explains his rejection of the church. " 'I wanted to be happy in this world, not out of it. . . . The white folks like for us to be religious, then they can do what they want to with us' " (p. 302).

In Malamud's fiction the opposite is true. Gentiles pressure Jews to abandon their faith. Contemporary Russian officials in "Man in the Drawer" outlaw the sale of religious articles, forbid the manufacture of matzohs, censor Jewish literature, and generally harass the religious. Judaism threatens the Bolshevik anti-Semites as much as it did their tzarist forerunners. In *The Fixer* the latter would like nothing better than to eliminate the Jews by extermination or conversion. In a scene reminiscent of *Native Son,* Bok is visited by a priest who tries to convert him. Although he rejects the overture, his actions differ from those of Bigger Thomas, who first passively accepts the cross and then dashes it to the floor. Bok neither submits nor violently rebels. Like the atheist in "Man in the Drawer," he quietly dons the prayer shawl and phylactery and ignores his enemies. The results are electrifying. The priest, resembling Dracula confronted by a cross, "holds his handkerchief to his mouth and retreat[ing] to the metal door, bang[s] on it with his fist" (p. 237). Bok, of course, will be punished physically, but he has won a moral victory. He denies by affirming. When Wright's characters renounce Christianity, they are left without any spiritual support. " 'I reckon I believe in myself. . . I ain't got nothing else . . . I got to die' " Bigger tells Max (p. 358). When Bok resists the priest, he asserts his Jewish identity and is no longer alone nor afraid.

Richard Wright spent his whole life seeking a tradition which could give meaning to his life. His anger and despair partly reflect the failure of his quest. Bernard Malamud inherited a several thousand year old culture which allows him a "qualified optimism" in the face of disaster. "I wondered," asks Wright, "if clean, positive tenderness, love, honor, loyalty . . . were native with man. I asked myself if these human qualities were not fostered, won, struggled, and suffered for, preserved in ritual from one generation to the next" (*Black Boy,* p. 33).

3

Fathers, Sons, and Lovers

> The Jewish family is above all historically a
> protective center.
> Frederick J. Hoffman, *The Modern Novel in
> America.*

> The 'peculiar institution' [slavery] also did vio-
> lence to the Negro family . . . no legal obstacle
> prevented the separation of slave 'husbands' and
> 'wives' or parents and children.
> Weisbord and Stein, *Bittersweet Encounter.*

Much of twentieth-century American fiction depicts a rapidly
changing, highly competitive, materialistic society which challenges
traditional male-female relationships and family allegiances. Men and
women exchange roles: Carrie Meeber supports her weak and
indecisive bigamist husband George Hustwood; pregnant Lena
Grove pursues her irresponsible lover Lucas Burch. Husbands and
wives betray each other and escape punishment: Daisy and Tom
Buchanan typify the new "morality." Children are alienated from
indifferent parents: Orphan Huck Finn becomes neglected Holden
Caulfield, refugee from boarding school life. Self-indulgence seems to
erode loyalty, respect, and responsibility, cornerstones of stable
families.

At first glance old institutions appear to have crumbled completely. But on closer inspection disintegration is balanced by the
possibility of regeneration, sometimes within the same work. Exposed to death and suffering, Nick Adams is comforted by his
understanding father, who makes his son's initiation less painful.
Rabbit Redux concludes with a weary Harry and Janice Angstrom
reunited after a series of sordid affairs. Unwanted by Lucas Burch,
Lena and her baby find sanctuary with Byron Bunch whose own life

assumes meaning when he accepts responsibility for them. Thus twentieth-century American writers offer alternative visions. Many portray the loss of love, the dissolution of marriage, and the destruction of families. But some also suggest that commitment, enduring relationships, and love are possible if adequate sacrifices are made. For historical and sociological reasons, the former vision dominates Afro-American literature while the latter viewpoint characterizes Jewish-American writing.

In black fiction slavery and racism undermine traditional family life. Rarely are both father and mother present to provide a secure home for their children. Generally women must fulfill both roles. The Negro matriarchy already dominates William Wells Brown's *Clotel* (1853), in which a beautiful octoroon is resold into slavery and separated from her daughter whom she desperately tries to regain. The novel is a melodramatic tribute to maternal love and a harsh attack on white men ravaging black women. In our century Zora Neale Hurston's *Jonah's Gourd Vine* (1934) applauds the courage, fidelity, and strength of Lucy Pearson who tolerates her philandering husband and dies trying to keep the family together. Ernest Gaines's *The Autobiography of Miss Jane Pittman* (1971) spans the life of a more than hundred-year-old heroine who outlives her husbands and adopted sons. Like Faulkner's Dilsey, Jane is a noble figure who overcomes multiple hardships. Richard Wright's fiction crystallizes the irresolvable conflicts of black men and women who are pitted against each other by a racist society. Bigger Thomas, economically, psychologically, and socially emasculated, unleashes his rage against his mother, his sister, and his girlfriend. Love, respect, and trust cannot grow in the bleak slum environment of *Native Son* nor in most of Wright's works, as will be seen later.

Ironically, while racial intolerance emasculates Negro protagonists and weakens their families, religious freedom challenges traditional male-female relationships in Jewish-American literature. In a secular society "poppa" no longer automatically commands respect as spiritual leader and family head. The "shtetl" patriarch, revered for his knowledge and wisdom, is absent from Philip Roth's and Bruce Jay Friedman's works, where Jewish mothers control their gentle but ineffectual husbands and overprotect their children. A capitalistic America defeats Mr. Portnoy and produces his aggressive wife who is determined to see her only son prosper. America creates

Meg, the oversexed dynamo, who dwarfs her husband and over-whelms her son in *A Mother's Kisses*.

But the emasculation of men is by no means characteristic of all Jewish-American fiction. In Chaim Potok's *The Chosen* women play secondary roles. Rebbezin Saunders, a shadowy, domestic figure defers to the men she faithfully serves. The novel focuses on strong father-son relationships in the Malter and Saunders families where conflicts are resolved eventually through mutual respect and trust. Potok has been accused of creating a simple, sentimental world in which the family remains a source of strength. If the criticism is valid, it applies as well to Herbert Gold's *Fathers*, an autobiographical tribute to the author's father, Sam Gold, a self-made man. Though not religious, Mr. Gold emerges as the ruler of his family. His ambition, energy, and imagination enable him to succeed economically, to enjoy life fully, and to command admiration and respect. If Gold's and Potok's vision of family life is nonexistent in Afro-American literature, it is also somewhat unusual in Jewish-American fiction.

In literature a more representative Jewish-American family probably would be a cross between the Portnoys and the Saunders. Perhaps of all contemporary Jewish-American writers, Bernard Malamud depicts most subtly conflicts between men and women and the possibility of compromise. Reflecting the influence of Old World traditions and New World experiences, his fiction celebrates the seemingly indecisive, henpecked character who develops into a gentle but imperfect father figure. In most of Malamud's works (*The Tenants* and *Rembrandt's Hat* are two recent exceptions) a truce prevails between lonely, dissatisfied men and women like Frank Alpine and Helen Bober *(The Assistant)* who hunger for love and who share responsibility for their fates.

A member of an ethnic minority, Malamud recognizes, as does Wright, the importance of stable families in sustaining America's outsiders. But Malamud's modified patriarchy where men rule subtly and gently is absent from Wright's fiction in which black men, forced into a passive role in white society, physically and psychologically exploit the women who struggle to keep the family together. Lacking positive father figures, Bigger Thomas, Cross Damon, and Jake Jackson remain rebel "sons," striking out at their women—mothers, girlfriends, and wives—as well as against white America. Although also self-centered and immature, Malamud's victims feel remorse and seek to make amends to the women they hurt. Guilt-ridden at having "raped" Helen Bober, Frank Alpine dedicates himself to supporting her and her mother in *The Assistant*. Yakov Bok in *The Fixer* accepts partial responsibility for his poor marriage and adopts his wife's illegitimate child. Interestingly, while both rebels and victims come from broken homes, their development differs. Most of Malamud's protagonists encounter father figures who enable them to move beyond their passions and selfish desires. Unlike Wright's rebels, who flee responsibility, Malamud's characters often find peace within the family.

At the heart of Malamud's fiction is a reverence for the family, a fragile unit forged from affection, loyalty, and above all duty. Malamud's perspective reveals the importance of his own immigrant Jewish background. In a personal letter, he pays tribute to his parents as "compassionate" people who influenced him.[1] Although he emphasizes that his "father always supported" them, he describes both his parents as "hardworking." Reminiscent of the Bobers in *The Assistant,* the Malamuds worked together in the store and developed something of a partnership in their marriage as well as in their business. His father fulfilled the role of a gentle patriarch. He guided and supported the family with the assistance of his well-meaning but somewhat protective wife (whom the author remembers as fearful of "gypsies"). In their compassion, in their dedication to the family, and in their perseverance, the senior Malamuds resemble some of the author's couples who, despite difficulties, are bound to each other in relationships evocative of European Yiddish life.

In the life of the European "shtetl" the most important institution was the family because it eased loneliness, encouraged self-discipline, and above all, served God's will. As authors Mark Zborowski and Elizabeth Herzog indicate, "If a man is not a husband and a father, then he is nothing. A woman who is not a wife and mother is not a 'real' woman."[2] To ensure family harmony and stability, adultery was forbidden, divorce was discouraged (though not outlawed if the marriage was disastrous), procreation was required, and children were expected to honor their mothers and fathers. Beyond these values, Jewish men and women fulfilled distinctive but complementary roles. "The temporal, domestic responsibilities are mother's domain . . . . while the . . . father's realm is spiritual and intellectual. He has the official authority, the final word on . . . momentous matters. However, he may be advised or coached—or opposed—in private by the mother.''[3] In Yiddish culture father is revered as a wise patriarch who rules firmly but does not abuse his authority. In I. B. Singer's "The Little Shoemaker" Abba exemplifies such a father. He never uses the switch nor raises his voice, but he commands respect and devotion.

In America the Jewish father's power is eroded. No longer the distant scholar, the fountain of wisdom, he does not inspire awe as he used to. Toiling alongside him, his wife is emboldened to assert herself more openly. Instead of quietly advising him, she may loudly nag him. Nevertheless, at least in Malamud's fiction, the man still makes the important family decisions. In *The Assistant* Morris Bober quietly determines the family's fate. He hides unpleasant news from his wife, continues to operate the store the way he wants to, and ignores her complaints and demands. Ida realizes that the grocer is "a hard man to move. In the past she could sometimes resist him, but the weight of his endurance is too much for her now" (p. 8). When he decides to shovel snow, she cannot stop him, nor can she persuade him to take advantage of an unsuspecting refugee. Despite her fears, Morris retains his Italian assistant, Frank Alpine. But the grocer rules with a gentle hand. He accepts the changes initiated by his ambitious assistant, who remodels the store to improve profits. But even in this enterprise, Morris has the ultimate veto and refuses to sanction deceptive business practices. He is clearly the family head, mourning for his dead son, worrying about his daughter's future, guiding his young helper, and operating the store. Though an American citizen for many years, Bober resembles many Eastern European Jewish men in his idealism and in his relationship to the family. A poor provider, he nevertheless retains their compassion and loyalty. As the practical wife, Ida complains, but she also loves Morris and blames herself for his failure to become a druggist. Helen's daughterly devotion makes her sacrifice her education to help support the family. It also makes her initially avoid Alpine, a non-Jew, so as not to hurt her parents. Despite poverty and suffering, the Bobers remain a family. Not surprisingly, then, Bober's death creates a vacuum, which will need to be filled by Frank Alpine, who becomes a surrogate father.

Most of Malamud's older men try to protect and care for their women and children. In "Angel Levine" the old tailor labors to save his wife's life. In "Idiots First" Mendel wrestles with the Angel of Death to spare his son. In "Suppose a Wedding" Maurice Feuer, "a retired sick Jewish actor" (*Idiots First*, p. 171) tries to prevent his daughter from marrying the wrong man. Fathers like Morris Bober and Feld, the shoemaker in "The First Seven Years," make mistakes, but their errors are a consequence of love and concern. Thus, Feld attempts to undermine his daughter's relationship with a poor Jewish refugee. In *The Fixer* Shmuel, thinking of his daughter's best interests, urges Bok to marry her. Even though the marriage fails, he exerts himself to help his imprisoned son-in-law. Short on money, Shmuel, like Bober, tries to guide his "adopted" son to be a good person. Even Sam Pearl and Julius Karp, the insensitive and materialistic storekeepers in *The Assistant,* contrive to make their children happy. A gambler, Pearl makes enough money to send Nat to college while Karp uses his money to try to arrange for Louis to marry Helen Bober, whom Louis likes.

In "Glass Blower of Venice" Margherita pleads with Fidelman to leave her husband alone. Although Beppo is bisexual she still wants him since "in the eyes of God he's [her] husband. [Without him the] family is a mess. . . . He's a good provider and not a bad father when there are no men friends around to divert him from domestic life" (*Pictures of Fidelman*, p. 207). Recognizing that he is disrupting an imperfect but viable family, Fidelman leaves Beppo, the man he loves. In *A New Life* a similar respect for marriage and family life causes Levin to feel guilty about his affair with Pauline Gilley. Despite Gerald Gilley's many faults, he had married Pauline and supported her two adopted children. Furthermore, as Irving Malin suggests, Levin views Gilley as a father figure "who had favored him with a job" and "who instructs him in the ways of the academic world." Levin hesitates to destroy this family until he convinces himself "that Gilley is a sneak, not a correct master [who has] disturbed Pauline."[4] Only a really miserable, thoroughly hopeless marriage should be dissolved, and then, if there are dependents, the family must find another male head. Thus, Seymour Levin quickly assumes responsibility for Gilley's wife and children.

In Malamud's fiction it is rare, though not impossible, for men to desert or abuse their families. In "The Mourners" Kessler is an aging recluse who had abandoned his family years before. Oskar Gassner, "the German refugee," had fled Hitler and left his wife behind to die.

In *The Assistant* the tough, brutal Detective Minogue, who nearly kills his warped son, is probably Malamud's worst father figure, but he is also an exception. Most of Malamud's male characters learn to be responsible family heads. Those who do not, suffer severely. Kessler makes a pathetic figure as he confronts his past sins and hopeless future. Oskar Gassner, unable to forget his gentile wife, gasses himself to death. And Detective Minogue is tormented by his son Ward, a hard-core criminal resembling Bigger Thomas.

Generally the presence of responsible father figures distinguishes Malamud's fiction from Wright's, where American society discourages black men from assuming responsibilities for their families. Wright's own family, described in *Black Boy,* provides a striking contrast with Malamud's. To begin with, Wright's mother, a school teacher, was educationally and socially superior to the poor peasant she married. Such inequality, common enough in black novels,[5] usually resulted in poor marriages. Wright recalls his father as a silent, harsh man who made his family hate him. Unable to earn a decent living in Memphis, he deserted his wife and two young sons for another woman. When Richard and his mother reluctantly visited him to beg for money, Wright Sr. and his mistress taunted them. From age six, Wright was raised by different people. His overworked and impoverished mother placed him in an orphanage from which he fled. Later she turned to her family for help.

As a youth, the author was surrounded by strong-willed women—his mother, grandmother, Aunts Addie and Maggie—and deserted by vulnerable men—his father, who ran away, and his grandfather, who emotionally withdrew from the family, preferring to dream of the pension the government owed him. The only dependable father figure, Uncle Hoskins, was killed by whites coveting his business. The burden of sustaining the family fell to the women. Before she became ill, Mrs. Wright was breadwinner, disciplinarian, and educator, the source of financial, emotional, and intellectual support for her two sons whom she taught to be independent and tough. She never let them forget "that [they] had no father . . . [and] that their lives would be different from those of other children" (*Black Boy,* p. 14). Although unmercifully strict at times, Mrs. Wright also loved her children who in turn loved and feared her. Young Wright's relationship with other women was much more negative: the inflexible, stern Miss Simon, director of the orphanage, terrified him; Aunt

Addie, a sadistic school marm, enraged him; Granny, a religious fanatic, caused him to rebel against family regimen. Nevertheless the women tried to educate and support Wright. Consequently his attitude towards black women was ambivalent. He appreciated their efforts, respected their strength, and sympathized with their predicament. But he also feared them, resisted their control, and consequently never married a black woman.[6]

Similar attitudes and patterns are revealed in Wright's fiction. In *Native Son* no mention is made of Bigger Thomas's father. Mrs. Thomas cleans, cooks, manages on relief checks while her daughter attends sewing classes to learn a trade. Bigger and his brother Buddy live at home but do not contribute to the family, which is maintained by the women. Wright clearly sympathizes with the women, but he also understands Bigger's rebellion against his mother who repeatedly reminds him of his helplessness. " 'You the most nocountest man I ever seen in all my life,' " she tells him (p. 8). But he has heard " 'that a thousand times' " (p. 8) and resists his mother's attempt to make him into an Uncle Tom. In *The Outsider* Cross Damon is raised by his mother, an embittered lonely woman who seeks refuge in religion after her husband has deserted her and the child. Constantly informed that black men are untrustworthy and irresponsible, Cross is ill-prepared to become a good husband and father. In neither *Native Son, The Outsider,* nor *Black Boy* are there reliable black men who can serve as positive models for the protagonists. The only male authority figures are whites who generally strengthen the rebels' determination to be free at any cost.

One of the few exceptions to this pattern is Wright's later novel, *The Long Dream,* which depicts a middle-class black family headed by Tyree Tucker. The fact that Fishbelly, Tyree's son, does not resort to violence as Bigger and Cross do is a consequence of Tyree's presence and advice. But racism weakens Tyree's patriarchal position. Though he is loyal and responsible, he repeatedly compromises his dignity in order to enhance his fortune and safeguard his son. Thus, he earns Fishbelly's gratitude but in the end loses his respect, because he exploits other blacks and allows whites to insult him. The reverse occurs in *The Assistant* where Alpine despises Morris Bober at first, but gradually learns to respect his kindness and integrity. In some ways Bober and Tucker are similar: both worry about their children and yearn to be good fathers. The Jew adores his daughter, pines for his dead son, and finds a replacement in Frank Alpine. The black loves his only child and tries to teach him how to survive and succeed in the South. Both men have businesses which their sons will inherit. But here the similarities end, for Frank will embrace Bober's values, his generosity, honesty, and selflessness, while Fishbelly will reject Tyree's greed, perfidy, and selfishness. The businesses are symbolic of the two fathers and the lives they lead. The marginal grocery nourishes poor customers; the funeral home and whorehouses exploit them. The one deals in life, the other in death. Similarly Bober and Tucker instruct their charges in different manners. Frank learns from Morris's good example. The grocer rarely pressures him or raises his voice. On the other hand, Fishbelly is bullied by his well-meaning father who tries to toughen him to deal with life in the South. Sympathetic to Tyree's plight, Wright illustrates how America undermines black families by depriving Negro men of self-respect.

In "Down By The Riverside" the protagonist is unable to save his pregnant wife. Like Morris Bober, the good-natured, simple Mr. Mann is also a victim of bad luck. But while the grocer's problems are primarily economic and partly of his own making, the poor farmer and his family are destroyed by racism. Bober struggles to improve his family's living standards; Mann struggles to save his family's lives during a raging flood. Despite all his efforts, however, he cannot overcome white contempt for black life. The soldiers and doctors he encounters dismiss his wife as " 'sick bitch having a picaninny' " (*Uncle Tom's Children*, p. 73). Medical care is inferior and too late to do any good. In death as in life Lulu is granted no dignity; her body is "rolled . . . out" (p. 75) to join a pile of black corpses.

White lust also destroys Negro families and trust between black men and women. In "Long Black Song" a white travelling salesman seduces a frustrated young black woman. Silas, the cuckolded husband, is doubly humiliated—aware that he has not satisfied his wife and that he is powerless to protect her. Similarly, in *Black Boy* Wright recalls an incident when he found himself helpless to defend a Negro maid from an insulting slap on the buttocks. Even worse for Wright, she was not offended and would have thought him "foolish" (p. 174) had he tried to shield her. Wright's protagonists are made to feel impotent in the eyes of their women who must bear the brunt of their humiliation and who are blamed for the rebels' troubles. " 'It makes my blood boil,' " says Jake Jackson in *Lawd Today*, " 'to see a nigger woman grinning at a white man like they do. . . . The time they caught that nigger woman and white clerk in the office I was ashamed to look a white man in the face around here. I felt they were laughing at me' " (p. 122).

While white men freely exploit Negro women, black men can be castrated for even looking at white women. Perceived "as a threat to the white woman or rather . . . to the manliness of the white males,"[7] Negroes are diabolically ensnared and punished. Frequently white women act as lynch-bait, luring Negroes to their deaths. In *The Long Dream* Fish and his friends hide in the basement of the Tucker burial home and frighten young women as they pass overhead. When one white lady collapses hysterically, appearing to have an orgasm, the boys are terrified of being accused of rape. Their fears are legitimate, as later illustrated by the murder and mutilation of Chris, a black youth caught with a white prostitute. Brought to the Tucker funeral parlor, Chris's body is a reminder that death awaits black men who "violate the line the whites" have drawn (*The Long Dream*, p. 157). Even those who respect the sexual taboos may be trapped, as Fish is when the police frame him on charges of raping a white lady. Such an atmosphere produces men incapable of enjoying affectionate, stable relations with women.

"Rape," Bigger Thomas reflects, "was what one felt when one's back was against a wall and one had to strike out in self defense. . . . He was a long, taut piece of rubber which a thousand white hands had stretched to the snapping point and when he snapped it was rape" (*Native Son*, p. 193). Though Bigger's thoughts describe his attitude towards whites, they also apply to relations between black men and women. For many of Wright's men sex substitutes for love. The penis becomes a spear, a conqueror's weapon, an expression of masculinity. In *The Outsider* Cross Damon has a "drunken," intense, passionate affair with Gladys, a pickup, who makes "no demands [but] simply clings to him" (p. 48). In *Native Son* Bigger Thomas "takes" Bessie on the cold floor of an abandoned slum apartment. A "frenzied horse . . . rid[ing] roughshod" (p. 198) over the protesting Bessie, Bigger regards her as an object that he can manipulate for his pleasure and power. "He was enjoying her agony, seeing and feeling the worth of himself in her bewildered desperation" (p. 126). She exists to serve him just as he is expected to serve the white world.

Since Bigger never treats Bessie as a human being, he can crush her when she becomes a burden. Similarly, in *Lawd Today* Jake Jackson and his friends adopt the attitudes of the "master race" as they describe their sexual conquests and convince themselves that their women enjoy being beaten and demeaned. Even Tyree Tucker, the respectable family man in *The Long Dream,* keeps a mistress, owns a whorehouse (which burns down from his negligence), and imparts his sexual mores to his son. In an early scene Fishbelly discovers his father having sex with his mistress in the back of the funeral parlor and compares him to a "sleek, black . . . locomotive . . . crashing past . . . and hurtling" (p. 27) through a dark tunnel. Later Tucker takes his son to a whorehouse and advises him " 'a woman's just a woman and the dumbest thing on earth for a man to do is to git into trouble about one' " (p. 150). In Tyree's world, " 'women serve [men], give . . . pleasure, [and are appreciated as pieces of good] meat' " (p. 182).

Although considerably more gentle than Tyree, Fishbelly resembles his father in at least one way. He also needs a woman's helplessness to make him feel manly. Gladys, a near-white prostitute, appeals to him because of her color (which confers status) and her defenselessness. His decision to redeem her is comparable to Leo Finkle's action in Malamud's "The Magic Barrel." Both men choose to save women from wanton lives, but while love and a need to sacrifice motivates Finkle, power inspires Fishbelly. "Poor little Gladys [is] just a woman" who doesn't know much and who needs to be taught. Fish "relishes the power he has over her" (p. 209). He enjoys controlling her destiny, but unlike Finkle, he is not prepared to inconvenience himself, displease his father, and marry the girl.

Wright's own experience with black women depressed him. Intelligent and sensitive, he sought companionship and was offered sex. In *Black Boy,* he resists Bessie, a love-starved teenager, who offers herself, when they first meet. An archetype of Wright's young female characters, Bessie considers sex a commodity, a means to attract and hold a man, but the author was not interested in a girl with whom he had nothing in common. When he did take advantage of women, he suffered for it. In "The Man Who Went To Chicago," Wright describes the "commissions" he received as an insurance salesman when pretty black housewives would pay their premiums with their bodies (*Eight Men,* p. 228). Unlike most of his protagonists, he pitied the poor, illiterate women who demeaned themselves. According to biographer Michel Fabre, Wright's sexual attitudes were molded in part by his mother who "could appeal to his moral sense."[8] In addition, an older female relative had made the young boy feel guilty by "ask[ing] him to look at and touch her vagina."[9] Beyond these psychological explanations Wright possessed the desire, the strength, the will which enabled him to observe and record but also transcend his sordid environment. Although he vividly described the pathology of black couples, he also envisioned the possibility of love and respect between black men and women.

In a rare later story titled "Man Of All Work" (*Eight Men,* pp. 117–62), Wright depicts an affectionate, loving black family. Earlier problems like the emasculation of Negro men, sexual tensions between blacks and whites, and economic difficulties of Negro couples are treated humorously. Unable to get a job to support his family, Carl Owens impersonates his wife Lucy and applies for a position as a cook and housekeeper for the Fairchilds. Carl-Lucy is so successful that Mr. Fairchild (who is neither fair nor innocent) makes advances to him. The climax occurs when a jealous, irate Mrs. Fairchild discovers her husband with the "maid" and, accusing her employee of betrayal, shoots him. Fortunately the wound is not serious and Carl, who has been given $200 to forget the incident, can return to his family and meet the payment on his house. In this story Wright contrasts a warm, unselfish black couple with a neurotic, self-indulgent white one. Unlike most of Wright's rebels, Carl willingly shares child care and domestic chores with his wife. Inwardly secure, he can do "women's work" in order to sustain his family. Although a victim of poverty, he confronts his situation humorously and imaginatively. Consequently, his young son Henry is also affectionate and considerate. On the other hand, the wealthy Fairchilds are greedy and inconsiderate. The husband, a budding banker, drinks and is unfaithful to his vain wife. Treated like a "lily-white" princess, their one daughter Lily is spoiled and insensitive. As in Wright's other fiction, whites are portrayed as villains who make trouble for blacks who just want to survive. But Carl is fortunate, and at the end he is able to rejoin his wife. Unlike Wright's other protagonists, Carl can share her tears. In many ways he resembles Malamud's characters who feel responsible for the women with whom they become involved.

Sexual involvement, in particular, imposes heavy burdens on Malamud's characters. Seymour Levin *(A New Life)* is a three-time loser until he meets the right woman. In his first encounter a competitive Arab prevents the Jewish "schlemiel" from mating with a local waitress. In the second, Levin and Avis Fliss, a spinsterish English instructor, undress but are interrupted by the department chairman's arrival. When they resume making love, he discovers that she has a benign tumor and his desire turns to pity. Although Levin has a brief affair with an attractive student, "he feels no true affection for the girl, and that [is] enough to undo in the aftermath some of his pleasure" *(A New Life,* p. 154). Only when Levin falls in love with Pauline Gilley is he able to enjoy sex. The setting is pastoral, the mood romantic as they make love in a soft green forest, and afterwards share their pasts. The forest also is the setting for Yakov Bok's affair with Raisl in *The Fixer.* Although Bok does not mention love or marriage until Raisl later pressures him, he cares for her and considers their relationship permanent. "One·day in the woods," he reflects, "we became man and wife" *(The Fixer,* p. 210). Without love, or at least affection, sex is unholy, an expression of base desires corrupting both partners. Bok realizes this as he prepares to have intercourse with Zinaida, a cripple, whom he pities as Levin does Avis. When he discovers that she is menstruating, he interprets it as a sign not to proceed, that their relationship is "unclean" (p. 52). Proper timing and consideration for the loved one's desires are also important. In "Still Life" Fidelman prematurely ejaculates in Annamaria's hand and earns her disgust. Like Frank Alpine in *The Assistant,* he is too eager, too hasty, and deprives himself of fulfillment. Alpine's eagerness results in his forcing himself on Helen Bober and forfeiting her love.

Since rape is unusual in Malamud's fiction, the scene deserves closer analysis. Superficially Frank's actions parallel Bigger Thomas's violation of Bessie in *Native Son.* Both men are drunk and feel troubled. Frank has just been fired by Morris Bober who has discovered his assistant's dishonesty. Bigger (the object of a massive police search) is even more desperate. Both men release their tensions through intercourse with their unwilling girlfriends. But here the similarities end, for it is clear that Frank is motivated by a combination of love and lust, while Bigger simply uses Bessie as a sex object. He may feel momentarily sorry for her, but he doesn't express any love or remorse. "He [is] conscious of nothing . . . but . . . what he wanted." Afterwards, "he felt the tenseness flow gradually from him" (p. 198). Conversely, Frank repeatedly proclaims his love to Helen, trying to justify his actions and make her understand. Instead of fulfillment, he experiences a great loss, loss of Helen, of love, and of self-respect. More importantly, the two men have had different relationships with their girlfriends. Bigger has always been indifferent to Bessie's needs. He only visits her when he is in the mood for sex. He jeopardizes her safety by making her an accomplice to murder. Consequently, it is horrifying but not surprising, when, shortly after lovemaking, he concludes that she will become a burden, and he kills her. In contrast, Frank's feelings for Helen are ambivalent: he lusts for her but wants to protect her. In the park the roles are meshed when he defends Helen from Ward Minogue's attack but violates her himself. Contrite, Alpine makes amends by assuming responsibility for Helen and her mother and by being converted to Judaism.

In stark contrast to Wright's emotionally immature protagonists, Alpine, like many of Malamud's young men, develops from impetuous lover to dependable family head. At the novel's end, he no longer thinks of Helen lustfully, but considers her a "little sister" (p. 245), whom he protects and supports at the expense of his own economic well-being. In *A New Life* Seymour Levin's relationship with Pauline Gilley undergoes similar changes. Initially he desires her, but as he matures, sex becomes less important. Ultimately affection and moral obligations bind Levin to Pauline whom he agrees to marry "on principle" (p. 349). In *The Fixer* a blend of affection and passion bring Yakov Bok and Raisl together. But that is not enough to sustain a permanent relationship and overcome the inevitable obstacles and tensions confronting Malamud's couples. According to *Life Is with People,* "if two young people are appropriately mated, . . . joint responsibility will weld them into a perfect pair."[10] Honesty, understanding, a willingness to compromise and cooperate are necessary for good family life. Bok and Raisl expect more from each other than from themselves. When he fails to improve their economic condition and she is unable to bear him children, they grow bitter and the marriage disintegrates. But it is never too late to change. Thus, when Raisl visits Bok in prison, they are moved to pity and forgive each other. Perhaps for the first time they communicate, and there is a possibility that if Bok is freed, they will be reunited in a mature relationship, characterized by mutual consideration and responsibility. Bok's decision to give his name to Raisl's illegitimate child indicates that like Alpine and Levin, he has developed into a reliable family man.

Although most of Malamud's protagonists mature gradually, one is steadfast from the beginning. In "The First Seven Years" Sobel, the lonely concentration camp survivor, is willing to work for "stingy wages" (*The Magic Barrel*, p. 14) in order to earn the hand of the shoemaker's daughter. Matured by his experiences, Sobel, the assistant, waits patiently for young Miriam to become a woman. He communicates his love silently, through the language of the "heart" (p. 14), and she understands. Based on the biblical tale of Jacob and Rachel, the story illustrates the influence of traditional values, patience, respect, and self-discipline, on some of Malamud's men and women.

The pressures to value marriage and family life are religious and communal, a reflection of the society in which the characters live. In *The Fixer* when Raisl deserts Bok for another man, the rabbi and villagers consider her a "pariah" and " 'blame [her] for [Bok's] fate' " (p. 289). In *The Assistant* Frank Alpine's Catholic school training and Helen Bober's Jewish background make them interested in a serious relationship. An admirer of St. Francis, Frank identifies with the monk's loneliness and desire for a family.[11] When Alpine spies on Helen in the shower and later violates her, he is guilt-ridden at having betrayed his values and her principles. In *A New Life* the strait-laced academic community of the 1950s disapproves of Pauline's affairs with Duffy and Levin and makes her worry about humiliating her husband. No prude, Malamud understands his characters' attempts to fulfill themselves even at the expense of community or tradition. But he also reveals the difficulties in doing so. Though they have free will, Malamud's characters are also members of particular societies which affect their attitudes and actions.

Two recent works, *Rembrandt's Hat* and *The Tenants*, illustrate how relationships between men and women deteriorate in a rapidly changing, dissolute world. *Rembrandt's Hat*, a collection of short stories, includes "In Retirement" which portrays the anguish of an older man attracted to a young, promiscuous woman unaware of his existence. His love note is greeted with derision and flung cruelly in his direction. Another tale, "Notes From A Lady at a Dinner Party," recalls some themes explored in *A New Life,* but lacks the qualified optimism of the earlier work. Karla Harris, a young attractive professor's wife, throws herself at Max Adler, a former student of her aging husband. Although the similarities between Karla and Pauline Gilley are apparent and Max bears some resemblance to Levin, Professor Harris elicits sympathy which Gerald Gilley forfeits. Harris's only crime is that he is considerably older than his frustrated child-wife, who rebels against the patriarchal figure by flinging herself at available young men. But Karla is a tease and Max is rewarded with frustration and guilt for betraying his mentor. The story ends with Karla singing " 'love, marriage, happiness' " (*Rembrandt's Hat,* p. 161) as Max bids the Harrises good-bye and makes a quick exit. Apparently "love, marriage, happiness" are an unlikely combination in the skeptical seventies.

Love, loyalty, and trust are also absent from Malamud's latest novel, *The Tenants,* where the predominantly black ghetto community influences the weak Jewish protagonist. Harry Lesser's irresponsibility towards Irene, the Jewish girl he has stolen from a black writer, is untypical of Malamud's protagonists—Alpine, Levin, and Bok—who commit themselves to the women they love or once loved. But Harry is different: He hasn't had a religious "education" (p. 213) like Bok or Alpine, and as a self-centered writer, he has avoided involvement with others. Lacking a positive father figure—his father is described in a dream sequence as "an irritable old man in a tubular wheelchair" (p. 190)—Lesser is guided by a black writer, Willie Spearmint, and his Harlem friends. Lesser is an apt pupil and uses Irene as Willie had done.

Malamud's depiction of black sexual relationships and attitudes parallels Wright's. Both authors explore imaginatively the consequences of America's emasculation of black men. Willie and his friends can be mistaken easily for Wright's characters who are also insecure and who use sex as a weapon, the only source of power available to them. In *The Tenants,* as in Wright's fiction, women are victims of black men whom they must sustain financially and emotionally. Thus, Mary, a Negro woman, can confess to Lesser that he has not given her an orgasm, but she must feign a climax with her black boyfriend to reassure him of his manliness. In order to make

Spearmint feel like a black conqueror, Irene Belinsky bleaches her hair and changes her name to Bell (an allusion to Southern Belle). For Willie, Irene represents an income, a "sweet lay," and a victory over the white world (p. 160). Irene's remark that " 'loving a black man . . . [makes her] feel black' " (p. 120) succinctly describes a relationship which simultaneously invigorates and debilitates Willie who has become dependent on his white "bitch" (p. 146). Irene functions as both earth mother and Jezebel, combining the roles assigned to Wright's black and white women.

Abandoned by weak fathers and raised by strong mothers, most of Wright's protagonists expect maternal care as well as sex from their women. Thus, in *The Outsider* Cross Damon marries Gladys, who has satisfied him sexually and nursed him through pneumonia. But their marriage ends when she gives birth and must mother her children instead of her husband. At the beginning of their relationship, he is "flattered to discover that she [is] curious about his notions and [has] the good sense to listen quietly" to him. He is willing to stay with her as long as "she made no demands, imposed no conditions, set no limits" (p. 48). Cross enjoys feeling like a man but not acting like one and he easily slips into the role of spoiled son. Gladys becomes both lover and mother, a role Fishbelly's girlfriend also fulfills in *The Long Dream,* where she observes that Fish looks just " 'like a baby when [he] sleeps' " and reflects that " 'some woman's watched every man while he slept' " (p. 175). In *Native Son* Bessie mothers Bigger Thomas, caressing him, giving him warm milk, and helping him in his escape attempt.

However, such care and consideration generally are not reciprocated. At the first hint of responsibility, most of Wright's men panic, and their women are left to raise sons who resent them and who transfer their rebellion to all women. The sons repeat their fathers' mistakes. In *The Outsider* Cross withdraws from Gladys when she has their first child. An early scene symbolizes the relationship between Wright's men and women. While his wife endures the pains of childbirth, Cross goes on a drinking binge which ends with him bringing home a whore. In *Lawd Today* Jake Jackson beats his sick wife when she begs him for money to pay the doctor. Like Bigger Thomas, both men justify their actions by convincing themselves that they have no alternatives, that in fact they are doing their women a favor. Bigger can kill Bessie because he believes her life is miserable.

Jake persuades himself that money spent on Lil would be wasted. Reasoning that his wife will be happier without him, Cross Damon attempts to drive Gladys crazy so that she will release him. Similarly, without any qualms, he can abandon his pregnant young mistress. He even considers killing his white girlfriend Eva, the one woman he loves, in order to "guard her from the monstrousness of himself" (p. 301). Though he stops short of murder, he contributes to Eva's suicide by confessing his past crimes.

Abused by society, by their lovers, and husbands, Wright's women emerge as victims who tolerate much pain. Like Malamud's women, they desire love and devotion, but they have such low self-esteem and so few options that they settle for less. A bottle of whiskey and Bigger's warm body binds Bessie to her unfeeling boyfriend. In *The Long Dream* Emma Tucker meekly endures Tyree's promiscuity and bullying for many years until his death in a whorehouse unlocks her repressed hatred. Cross Damon's teenage mistress is a "passionate child" (*The Outsider*, p. 29) willing to trust a married man. Similarly Gladys is so grateful for Cross's attention that she forgives him his transgressions.

But there is a limit to the abuse Wright's women can tolerate. Ironically, they turn to white authorities for protection against black brutality. In self-defense Lil Jackson complains to her husband's white supervisors that he has beaten her. Similarly, Gladys Damon asks Cross's white boss to withhold his wages for child support. Both women resemble Wright's mother who, in *Black Boy,* appeals to a white judge to force her husband to provide for the children. In all three cases whites perfunctorily issue warnings which are promptly ignored by black men aware that the authorities are indifferent to the welfare of black families. Under such circumstances the women have no recourse but to defend themselves. After many beatings, Lil finally stabs Jake. When Cross assaults Gladys for the second time, she obtains a gun and threatens to shoot him. The rebels transform their good-natured, hard-working, patient women into embittered shrews. "This was a cold and vindictive Gladys," Cross reflects, "created by him" (*The Outsider*, p. 63).

Although Malamud's younger women are described repeatedly as "troubled, sad, [and] dissatisfied," they are more independent and idealistic than Wright's females. Depicted as "nagging wives . . ., the frequent bane of Jewish husbands"[12] they set high standards for themselves and their men. A typical Malamudian female, Helen Bober *(The Assistant)* dreams of escaping her impoverished environment through education and a good marriage. Both practical and romantic, Helen inherits her father's idealism and her mother's skepticism, which she seems unable to reconcile. She rejects a marriage proposal from Louis Karp, a wealthy merchant's son, is disillusioned by Nat Pearl, a law student only interested in sex, and she tries to remake Frank Alpine into an ideal husband. Helen regards sex as sacred, an expression of deep love and commitment. She refuses to allow herself to be used as Wright's women are. Although not a virgin, she will not have intercourse with Frank until she is certain of their love. After the rape scene, Frank must win back Helen by disciplining himself and loving her from a distance. In *The Fixer* Raisl feels guilty about her affair with Bok but refuses to marry him until he declares his love. Despite the fact that the fixer, unlike Wright's rebels, is a faithful, hard-working husband, Raisl grows dissatisfied with their humble life. In Wright's fiction men abandon women, in Malamud's women sometimes desert their men. Thus, Raisl leaves Bok when they no longer can communicate. In *A New Life* Pauline overcomes her own guilt and is unfaithful to Gerald, her devoted but insensitive husband. In search of love she is willing to sacrifice the economic security and community position unavailable to Wright's women. Like Helen Bober, Pauline is an idealist, for whom "love, marriage [and] happiness" should be inseparable. Consequently she seeks fulfillment through a permanent relationship with Levin.

In *The Tenants* Irene expects more from Harry whom she believes dependable than from Willie whom she pities. Before she becomes involved with Harry, he must declare his intentions to marry her, and even then she hesitates, afraid that he will (like her black lover) exploit her. She demands a future with him and insists that their love take precedence over his writing. Quickly Irene changes from Willie's patient, long-suffering mistress (resembling Wright's women) into Harry's nagging fiancee, from a confused, stage-struck girl into a middle-class Jewish woman. She objects when Harry uses the word "bitch" which she accepts as part of Willie's vocabulary. Underneath her bohemian clothes she is a typical Malamudian female—with sad, "troubled eyes" *(The Tenants,* p. 42)—hungering for a meaningful life. Had Harry been more like Levin, he might have sacrificed his freedom and career, married Irene and accepted the responsibilities of a family man. But Harry is too self-centered and the disappointed Irene leaves.

However, many of Malamud's women are as capable of change and compromise as his men are. In fact, like Wright's women, they are molded by their relationships with men. Irene will not return to Harry because she realizes his work is more important than she is. On the other hand, Pauline vows to be " 'a good wife' " (*A New Life*, p. 366) to Levin who has sacrificed his career for her, unlike Gerald Gilley, who is preoccupied with his work. In *The Fixer* Raisl visits Bok in prison and begs him to come home after he shows his love by assuming responsibility for her baby. Although tensions still exist between Helen Bober and Frank Alpine in *The Assistant,* there is a suggestion that they will stay together. By the novel's end, as previously mentioned, Frank has completely reformed and dedicated himself to supporting the Bober women. Helen, in turn, concedes that she may have judged him too harshly. In all these cases men and women affect each other's behavior but the success of their relationships depends on the men.

In "Still Life" Arthur Fidelman, earlier having earned Annamaria's contempt, learns to postpone sexual satisfaction in order to combine the roles of lover and father. "In a final tableau the physical and moral mingle grotesquely," as Annamaria, a guilt-ridden Catholic, confesses her sins to Fidelman ("dressed up to paint himself as priest") and begs him to save her.[13] Their roles have been reversed. No longer the impatient lover, Fidelman, now father confessor, orders the frantic Annamaria to undress and then "pumping slowly nail[s] her to her cross" (*Pictures of Fidelman,* p. 68).

Frequently children provide the means to reconcile Malamud's men and women and help them to mature. In Malamud's fiction fertility is a blessing; in Wright's it is a curse. Thus, while both Yakov Bok and Cross Damon are pushed into marriages for which they are not ready, the former suffers because his wife is barren; the latter because his wife gives birth. At the end of *The Outsider* Damon refuses to acknowledge his tearful children whom he is forced to confront in court. "Those frightened, little brown-faced boys were his sons," he reflects. "They were the future of himself [but] he had rejected that self" (p. 359), thus condemning them to hopeless lives. Near the end of *The Fixer* Bok agrees to give his name to Raisl's illegitimate baby, appropriately called Chaiml (life). For it is Chaiml who reunites Raisl and Bok and restores purpose to the fixer's life. Damon, the rebel, welcomes an accident which frees him from his family; Bok, the victim, desires freedom so he can provide for his wife and son. With his father-in-law Shmuel dead, Bok must replace him' and wholeheartedly become a father. " 'Whoever acts the father is the father' " Raisl has told him and, according to Malamud, she is right. In a dream sequence the fixer confronts Tzar Nicholas, "Little Father," who asks him if he is a father. " 'With all my heart,' " replies Bok, accusing the Tzar of being a poor patriarch, depriving Russia of justice and hope. A haemophiliac, the Tzar's son Alexis symbolizes Nicholas's failings, a lack of " 'charity [and] respect for the most miserable.' " Shmuel had once observed similar flaws in Bok, but the fixer, unlike the Tzar, admits his mistakes and becomes a responsible father.

" 'Whoever acts the father is the father' " also describes Seymour Levin's development in *A New Life*. Like Alpine and Bok, Levin has been orphaned. His own painful childhood makes him feel compassion for the adopted Gilley children even before he falls in love with their mother. In fact, his need for a family attracts him to both. Later he confronts a predicament similar to Cross Damon's. Penniless and unemployed, he discovers that Pauline is pregnant, and though he no longer loves her, he cannot leave her. While Damon tries to convince Dot, his mistress, to have an abortion, Levin rejects the idea and instead decides to marry Pauline. His decision is influenced by his reverence for life and by Pauline's refusal to pressure him. Because both respond unselfishly, showing concern for the other's fate, the "new life" brings them together.

But, of course, Malamud's characters have not experienced slavery and racism. Even in *The Fixer* where anti-Semitism is pervasive, the "shtetl" still provides a sanctuary which nurtures the family. Unfortunately Wright's characters have no refuge; America becomes one vast concentration camp in which many black families are systematically destroyed. Ironically, the search for the promised land hastens the disintegration of black life, as shall be seen in chapter 4.

4

The Promised Land

Perhaps never in history has a more unprepared folk wanted to go to the city; we were barely born as a folk when we headed for the tall and sprawling centers of steel and stone . . . We, who had had our personalities blasted with two hundred years of slavery, had been turned loose to shift for ourselves.

Richard Wright, *Twelve Million Black Voices*

But at night remembrance of New York City struck him like a spear hurled across the continent. . . . Sometimes he thought of it as a jeweled grave to fall into, or a wound at his side. At night he missed the movement and mystery of people in dark city streets.

Bernard Malamud, *A New Life*

As a dominant theme in American literature, the search for the promised land reflects the restlessness, ambition, and optimism of a people who had severed their bonds with the Old World and settled a virgin land with a seemingly endless frontier. Although the quest often ended in failure, the journey motif became firmly established in American fiction as numerous protagonists sought prosperity and freedom in new surroundings. Some novels—*O Pioneers!*, *My Antonia, Giants in the Earth*—record the pioneers' epic struggles to tame the West. In other—*Winesburg, Ohio; Sister Carrie; The Great Gatsby*—protagonists exchange small town life for the sophisticated city which tests their integrity. At times the pursuit of elusive fulfillment transports individuals to Europe in search of culture, tradition, and an understanding of their origins. Similar odysseys are described in Afro-American and Jewish-American fiction where the protagonists' distinctive histories determine the pattern of wandering and its eventual outcome.

In black literature flight becomes an end in itself as characters journey North or in some cases to Europe but are unable to find a permanent home. "Oppression makes the Negro an exaggerated American—[with] the problems of all other [Americans] only more naked and obvious."[1] Like the "Ancient Mariner," Negro characters seem condemned to roam the earth, reliving and retelling their experiences wherever they go. The city which promises freedom and opportunity proves unsuitable for a rural, peasant folk whose color creates an additional barrier. In Europe educated Negroes are patronized but never really assimilated, and Africa is too culturally removed to provide a sanctuary for most American Negroes. Nor can black protagonists find refuge by returning to their birthplace. Home—the rural South—combines the fragrance of magnolias with the terror of a lynch mob. Even in Jean Toomer's *Cane,* where rural Georgia is the source of black vitality, the journey South is difficult and dangerous, requiring more fortitude than the urbanized protagonist possesses. In Nella Larsen's *Quicksand* an educated mulatto travels to New York, to Europe, and finally back to the rural South, which suffocates her spirit. A similar odyssey occurs in *The Autobiography of an Ex-Colored Man,* where the protagonist's only option is to pass as a white man in a northern city. William Attaway's *Blood on the Forge* is representative of novels which condemn the industrialized North but recognize the impossibility of returning to the oppressive South. American racism "keeps the Nigger running" and denies him a promised land.

The wandering black Americans confront a situation more desperate than that of American Jews, who possess a spiritual homeland in Palestine and who find refuge in the United States. Following in the Pilgrims' footsteps, Jewish protagonists seek prosperity and liberty in America. Despite some difficulties, they possess urban backgrounds and thus adapt more successfully to the cities which are so destructive of black life. In earlier immigrant novels like Abraham Cahan's *The Rise of David Levinsky* and Ludwig Lewisohn's *The Island Within,* characters succeed economically but pine for the "shtetl" life they have left behind. America becomes the golden calf which exacts spiritual sacrifices, but the choice is the protagonists' who are free to act differently and sometimes do. In more recent novels the spiritual homeland is transferred to American urban ghettos which can be cruel but which claim the loyalty of Jews.

In *Fathers* Herbert Gold reveals his affection for Cleveland where he grew up and for San Francisco where he now lives. Although the protagonist in Chaim Potok's *The Chosen* leaves the sheltered community of Chasidic Williamsburg, the teeming streets and close-knit neighborhood continue to exert a positive influence on him. Even in Michael Gold's *Jews Without Money,* a protest novel of the 1930s, in which the city crushes the weak, the Lower East Side also fosters communal bonds and sustains Jewish life which is dissipated in Bruce Jay Friedman's and Philip Roth's gilded suburban ghettos. Unable to share blacks' attachment to the soil, Jews are rooted in urban communities. Nature offers a respite from daily pressures but never a permanent home. Saul Bellow's Herzog may seek refuge in the countryside, but he is still an urbanite, destined to return to bustling, neurotic Chicago.

In Afro-American fiction flight leads nowhere, as Ralph Ellison suggests in his perceptive essay "Harlem Is Nowhere." In Jewish-American fiction it educates the protagonist and brings him home. The contrast is evident in Richard Wright's and Bernard Malamud's works, in which wandering blacks and Jews search for their promised land. Wright depicts the Negro migration from rural South to urban North where oppressive indifference can be as harmful as Southern barbarity. Despite slavery and Jim Crowism, the black community is strongest in the South. *Uncle Tom's Children* and *Black Boy* reveal communal bonds absent from the author's urban fiction. But white persecution forces Wright's characters to flee the South and deprives them of their roots as their African ancestors had been. The "promised land" of the North is a wasteland, destroying black spirit and hope. Like trapped animals, black characters become ensnared in concrete jungles, and are finally exterminated as the hunters close in. While Wright's rebels are uprooted peasants seeking freedom and opportunity in cities which ignore them, Malamud's victims are frequently restless ghetto dwellers who, driven by their desire for a better life, leave their homes only to return with a new perspective. Some, like Yakov Bok in *The Fixer,* travel a short distance from small village to big city (paralleling the movements of American Negroes). Others like Alpine, Levin, and Fidelman cross continents and oceans but inevitably are drawn back to their origins. Both the authors' own journeys and their protagonists' odysseys suggest that while blacks remain homeless, Jews have ceased their wandering.

In *Twelve Million Black Voices* Wright recorded the "complex movement of a debased feudal folk toward a twentieth century urbanization" (p. 93). Described in *Black Boy* and several recent biographies, Wright's life reflects a migratory pattern which began in rural Mississippi and ended in cosmopolitan Paris. A desire to escape persecution and humiliation caused him first to leave the South and later the nation. The decision was not easy, for it is apparent that he thought of himself as an American and also missed the South[2] whose beauty and folk culture he describes in *Black Boy, Uncle Tom's Children,* and *The Long Dream.* Just as New York City is home to Malamud and his characters, the rural South holds a special place in Wright's fiction. Although the "nightmarish landscape" haunts the author with its scenes of degradations, castrations, and lynchings, there is another attractive, almost seductive side to the South, a world of "morning dew . . . , wet, green garden paths . . . , dreamy Mississippi waters . . . , of wild geese and sugar cane," and hovering over all "the blood-red glare of the sun's afterglow" (*Black Boy,* p. 7). It was the South's lushness which nurtured Wright and which he was forced to leave but never forgot, as his fiction repeatedly illustrates.

Wright's reluctant exile began when he was a child and his family moved to Memphis, a move he blamed for destroying his parents' marriage and reducing him to a humiliating existence. Like most southern cities, Memphis combined the evils of rural racism and urban depersonalization. It was only a matter of time before Wright fled North, seeking freedom first in Chicago and then in New York—cold, cosmopolitan centers, where he grew artistically and intellectually but never felt at ease. In the northern cities he observed the "violence, poverty and alienation" (*Twelve Million Black Voices,* p. 136) which destroyed blacks like Bigger Thomas, Jake Jackson, and Cross Damon. Artistic success permitted Wright to continue his "quest" for human dignity in Paris, where he settled eventually. But acceptance by Parisian intellectuals could not satisfy Wright's curiosity about his origins, which brought him to Ghana, where, as mentioned in chapter 2, he remained a stranger despite his blackness. His travels through the United States, Europe, and West Africa underscore his restlessness and contrast with Bernard Malamud's journeys.

Born in Brooklyn, New York, Bernard Malamud also has travelled widely but has always returned to the United States and still maintains an apartment in New York City, spiritual center for the author and his characters. Although the city can be cruel to Malamud's victims, it sustained a viable Jewish community which nourished the author. Malamud's New York can be depressing, but it is rarely impersonal. Instead of flashy billboards and tall skyscrapers there are small shops and busy streets, alive with talking, gesturing Jews who may be poor but who can still dream of a better future for their children. While Wright had to use subterfuge to borrow books from a Memphis library, Malamud was able to get a free education at City College and to continue his studies at Columbia University. Until almost forty, Malamud remained in New York where he wrote and taught. His decision to accept a position at Oregon State University was not prompted by fear or persecution but by a desire for a change. His journey (a reversal of Wright's migration) took him from an urban community to a rural town where he stayed for about ten years. Although enthralled with the countryside, he was an outsider in rural Oregon. Since Malamud needed kindred spirits with whom to socialize, he accepted a teaching position at Bennington College, a cosmopolitan New England school within several hours driving distance from New York. Periodic trips to Europe have provided material for *Pictures of Fidelman* and *The Fixer,* but unlike Wright who remained in exile, Malamud always returns home to the United States.

Both authors' journeys provide models for their restless protagonists, whose flights illuminate their environment and personalities and thus deserve closer analysis. Why do Malamud's victims and Wright's rebels leave their birthplaces? What are they searching for and what do they find? Certainly persecution causes some of the black and Jewish characters to flee. In Wright's short story "Big Boy Leaves Home" the protagonist observes his friend being burned and castrated and realizes that his fate will be the same unless he escapes the white lynch mob. Pursued by hound dogs, Big Boy is helped by the black community and, like thousands of runaway slaves, is secretly transported North. A closing image of Big Boy subsisting on crumbs of corn bread and cold water as he lies hidden beneath the truck's trapdoor is prophetic of the bleak, prison-like existence awaiting him in the North, an existence shared by Wright's urban rebels. As the truck speeds northward, "the corn bread crumbs . . . [are] shaken out of his bosom . . . [and blended with] splinters and sawdust in the golden blades of sunshine" (*Uncle Tom's Children*, p. 53), an indication that Big Boy has been separated permanently from the family and community which have succored him.

Big Boy's flight is closely paralleled by Fishbelly Tucker's decision to leave the South at the end of *The Long Dream*. Although Tyree Tucker has money, it cannot save him from being murdered by a police chief who fears exposure of his corruption. As discussed in chapters 1 and 3, Fish realizes that it is only a matter of time before he tangles with the police and suffers a similar fate. With six thousand dollars from his father's illegal businesses, he steals away, taking a plane to New York and from there on to France, a country that a black soldier friend has described as "no heaven . . . [but a place where] folks just more like real human beings than them crackers . . . in Mississippi" (p. 372). Fish's European journey is not undertaken for economic advancement since he leaves behind his father's "business" but represents his attempt to survive, to escape death. Wright suggests that Europe and the United States are viewed differently by white and black Americans. On the plane Fish is seated next to a young white man who has promised his Italian immigrant father that he will return to the old country to see the "poverty and ignorance" for himself and thereby be better able to appreciate America, the land his father had called his "wonderful romance" (p. 379). Later Fish reflects that "that man's father had come to America and found a dream; he had been born in America and had found a nightmare." He also wonders whether he will "ever find a place that he could call 'My wonderful Romance' " (p. 380).

Some of Malamud's characters emigrate for the same reason. In "The German Refugee" Oskar Gassner, a noted "Berlin critic and journalist," is driven out by the rise of Nazism (*Idiots First*, p. 196). But while Wright's characters have only known bondage, Gassner and other refugees had been "accomplished" (p. 196) and respected members of German society until Hitler had "destroyed [their] careers, [and] uprooted [their lives]" (p. 203). Emigration saves them but adjustment to a strange land and lower standard of living is difficult. Still, the United States offers a sanctuary and if the refugees do not succeed, it is not the country's fault. Gassner's suicide is not prompted by life in America where he finds friends and a new career, but by his guilt at having abandoned his German wife.

In *The Assistant* Morris Bober must assume responsibility for his economic failure. Although "he had hoped for much in America and got little," Morris realizes that "he and the bloodsucking [grocery] store" have deprived his family of a better life (p. 27). In a conversation with Frank Alpine he describes his flight from Russian poverty and anti-Semitism as the high point of his life. Unfortunately the grocer is not tough enough to succeed in a capitalistic society and his hard-won freedom is eroded as he imprisons himself in the store (described in chapter 1). But if Morris is crushed in America, other Jewish immigrants are not. While America adopts a conscious, deliberate policy of repression towards Wright's black rebels, she treats Malamud's characters neutrally, allowing some, like Karp and Pearl, to thrive, others, like Bober and his friends Breitbart and Marcus, to fail. To some extent Malamud is critical of a country where honesty and virtue are not materially rewarded, where "one man counted for nothing" (p. 206), but conditions elsewhere are much worse and Bober is able to retain his humanity, which many of Wright's characters cannot do. The latter, who are denied basic liberties, struggle to live and need money to buy protection from American racists. Tyree Tucker builds an illegal black empire which temporarily frees his son from jail; Julius Karp, whose freedom is secure in America, is a greedy capitalist. Morris recognizes this and chooses not to imitate Karp and his other successful Jewish neighbors. America permits him this choice. If migration does not materially improve Bober's life, it is because he recreates the old world in the new. Morris expects bad luck and is not disappointed, even experiencing anti-Semitism in his adopted country. But the anti-Semitism is a consequence of one individual's ignorance; it is not government policy like that which oppresses Yakov Bok in Russia.

The fixer, whose situation most closely resembles that of Wright's characters, leaves his rural "shtetl" to escape past humiliations and poverty. Unlike some of Wright's protagonists who entertain illusions about the promised land of the North, Bok recognizes that Kiev may be dangerous, that he may encounter the anti-Semitic "Black Hundreds" there or be engulfed by the Jewish ghetto's poverty. Still, he is determined to go to Kiev, and Bok decides that if he fails, he can always emigrate to America. Surprisingly, the fixer does well in the Russian city, where he passes as a gentile and through a chance meeting and hard work becomes a brickyard overseer, a supervisory position unavailable to Wright's characters. Although Bok's good fortune is only temporary, his journey to the city is not futile, for there he learns to appreciate his birthplace and his history.

By contrast, most of Wright's rebels drift aimlessly until they are destroyed. In "The Man Who Killed A Shadow," Saul Saunders "lives with his grandmother who moved constantly from one small Southern town to another [so that] even physical landscapes . . . have . . . little emotional meaning for [him]" (*Eight Men,* p. 194). Lacking economic opportunity and roots, Saul wanders from job to job until he becomes a janitor in a church, where, no longer able to elude the white "shadows" which haunt him, he kills one and then, weary of fleeing, resigns himself to death. Saul's aimlessness parallels Bigger Thomas's in *Native Son.* From the moment Bigger awakens, he is in constant motion, but it is movement without purpose. He chases, corners, and kills a rat, which will be replaced most likely by another one. In the streets he joins other youths with no place to go and nothing to do. Dreaming of escape, he admires a pigeon gracefully evading an oncoming car; and he envies the white pilots soaring above his ugly environment. But poverty and race shackle Bigger to his grim surroundings until he kills and then must dodge the authorities. In book 2 of *Native Son,* appropriately titled "Flight," Bigger struggles heroically to escape his persecutors, but he is no more successful than the rat he slaughters at the beginning of the novel. Like Saul Saunders, he ends by accepting death. Wright makes it clear, however, that other Biggers will take his place.

In *Lawd Today* Jake Jackson distinguishes between constructive movement and purposeless motion. " 'Them white boys,' " he observes in the post office, are " 'always in a hurry to get somewhere,' " and they will. ' "But a nigger just stays a nigger' " (p. 103). Jake and his friends hardly remain stationary, but they are on a treadmill. Part 2—"Squirrel's Cage"—aptly describes the assembly line post office, where black workers are forced to work like robots without any satisfaction or rewards. Under close supervision blacks monotonously sort mail whose contents and destinations are unknown. The work appears meaningless. " 'It's hard to just move your hands all day and not see what you are doing. . . . This kind of work can drive a guy nuts' " (pp. 130–31), they remark, aware that they are trapped. At the day's end the cage opens and the "squirrels" seek temporary relief in dingy bars and brothels, described in part

3—"Rat's Alley." However, their frenetic attempt to enjoy themselves fails, and weary and defeated, they crawl home to their holes.

Some of Wright's more imaginative protagonists do try to change
environments. Fishbelly, as previously noted, has the money to leave
America. Since the sequel to *The Long Dream—Island of
Hallucinations*—has never been completed, Fish's life as an expa-
triate remains uncertain. But according to Michel Fabre Wright's
notes indicate parallels between Fishbelly's and Wright's experiences.[3] Cross Damon's fate, however, is known. In many ways he
resembles Malamud's younger characters—Alpine, Levin, and
Fidelman—all of whom are dissatisfied with life and try to escape past
mistakes and present troubles. A desire to flee marital and financial
responsibilities prompts Damon to take advantage of a train accident,
and, like Bok, to hide his identity by moving to another city. *The
Outsider* records his desperate quest for freedom and dignity. Like his
author, Damon knows no peace and is unable to assuage his restlessness. Exhausted from running, he finally submits to the early death
awaiting most of Wright's urban rebels.

Damon's city is similar to Jake Jackson's in *Lawd Today* and
Bigger Thomas's in *Native Son*. Inhospitable, it offers no shelter from
cruel weather and unrelieved poverty. In "The Man Who Went To
Chicago" Wright describes the North's frigid climate which adds to
the Negroes' woes. "The house," he writes, "was as cold to me as
the Southern Streets had been in the winter" (*Eight Men*, p. 210). In
Lawd Today Jake and his friends enjoy an uncommonly warm
February day in Chicago and pine for the "soft . . . warm [Southerly]
air . . . and the evening sun . . . red like blood" (*Lawd Today*, p. 154).
The unpredictable northern climate afflicts them as it does many of
Malamud's characters and reflects their uncertain fortunes. As they
vent their frustration through gambling, drinking, and whoring, the
sun quickly disappears and is replaced by ice and snow. Penniless,
they are tossed onto the cold streets after a barroom brawl. "The
end," as Morris Bober would say, "fitted [their] day" (*The Assistant*,
p. 27).

The city's ruthlessness permeates *The Outsider*, which opens
with Cross and his friends fighting the cold, snowy Chicago air as they
leave work. Later, in New York, where Cross's problems escalate,
the snowflakes turn into a "blizzard" as he searches through a
graveyard for a new identity. Quite emphatically Wright identifies the

"cemetery [with] the snowflakes . . . , the white marble crosses [with] the white shroud of snow" (p. 138). Cross's father had been wounded in a street brawl and left to die in "sub-zero weather" in a vacant Harlem lot (p. 21), a fate which his son will suffer. "Shivering . . . and covered with snow" (p. 139), Damon also resembles Bigger Thomas whose flight from the police leads him to the icy rooftops of South Side tenements. Once again the bitter cold is symbolic of the death which awaits Bigger, who will be captured shortly and sentenced to die. In both *Native Son* and *The Outsider,* northern cities are characterized as cold and impersonal bastions, where white people and frosty climate conspire to destroy Negroes. Only alcohol and sex can warm Wright's benumbed characters who cannot ignore the contrast between black and white life in "the Promised Land" (*Lawd Today,* p. 154).

In the white world which Bigger invades "the houses [are] huge; lights glow softly in windows [and] the streets are empty, save for an occasional car" (*Native Son,* p. 37). It is "a cold and distant world . . . of white secrets carefully guarded" (p. 37), a world very different from the one Bigger and Cross have known. In their section there is no privacy. Bigger lives with his mother, sister, and brother in one decrepit, harshly lit room with not even a place for the women to undress. Later, as he hides from the police, he spies on a black family of five crowded together in a room much like his own. The lack of privacy—husband and wife copulating while the children watch—is all too familiar to Bigger and Wright's other urban dwellers. Cross's mother lives in a "tiny, shabby room" typical of those in Chicago's and Harlem's "rows of [drab] tenements" (p. 126) as indistinguishable from each other as their inhabitants are. In such areas Wright's rebels must struggle to preserve their individuality against the anonymity bestowed by poverty and overcrowding. The more hemmed in they feel, the more, like rats in a maze, they fight to escape, frequently destroying others in the process. Clearly, Wright condemns the city, as Dreiser had done, for its dehumanizing effects. Harlem and the South Side are held responsible for the rebels' murderous actions, which occur less frequently in the South where Negroes are comforted by the rich earth, warm sun, and open spaces which foster more of a sense of community.

Only Wright's southern tales contain heroic blacks—Reverend Taylor in "Fire and Cloud," Aunt Sue in "Bright and Morning Star,"

Brother Mann in "Down By The Riverside"—who sacrifice for their family and community. The passionate, blood-stained land inspires some of Wright's characters in a way the North cannot. Thus, in "Fire and Cloud," the Reverend Taylor, depressed by the sufferings of his starving congregation, is comforted by memories of a better time when he "had walked behind his plow, between the broad green earth and a blue sweep of sunlit sky [and had known] the earth was his and he was the earth's" (*Uncle Tom's Children*, p. 132). On such land "he had first taken . . . a wife . . . [and had watched] his first-born son . . . growing to a strong, upright manhood" (p. 130). The soil had nourished Taylor, enabling him to preach, and later to challenge the town's white authorities. A close relationship with nature had strengthened his ties with his fellow men.

While Wright's northern rebels are self-centered and devious, some of his southern characters courageously defend their loved ones. In "Bright and Morning Star" Sue is willing to sacrifice her life to protect her Communist comrades and to avenge her son. A monumental earth-mother, she envelops her sons in "the charm and magic of her vision" (*Uncle Tom's Children*, p. 184), and inspires admiration in the white girl who loves her son. Nobly rendered, Sue's death contrasts with that of Bigger and Cross who die alone and frightened. Sue, however, is killed with her son on southern soil and dies secure in the knowledge that she has saved others. "Buried in the depths of her star, swallowed in its peace and strength, [she does] not feel her flesh growing cold" (p. 215) as Cross does. Instead her body blends with the "rich black earth" (p. 181) which fortified her; she becomes like the North Star, a guiding light for others.

Some of Wright's southern folk endure in a way that his other characters do not. They are the real heroes of his fiction. In "The Man Who Saw The Flood" a black peasant family return to their water soaked land after a ravaging flood. A certain stoicism prevails as the family gives thanks that a few possessions—a stove, the water pump, some tobacco—were spared. Although much else was destroyed, and their food is gone, Tom and his wife resign themselves to starting over again, aware that they will be further in debt to the white man. It is as if the people and the land are one in their determination to persevere, to recover, and sustain life. In the countryside the ruinous floods and yellow mud are followed by a "high, blue sky, full of white clouds and sunshine. A gusty spring wind" (*Eight Men*, p. 111) gives hope to the family who, like Noah and his kin, has survived the worst and returns to till the soil. Those who remain in the rural South sometimes perish, but their lives are marked by a courage and commitment which Wright's northern characters lack. In "Down By The Riverside" nature and white men conspire to destroy Brother Mann, who struggles valiantly to survive and to save his family. Love for his farm keeps him from leaving during a flood; love for his family makes him battle the raging waters and the white authorities. Although he loses, Mann exhibits the same bravery as Aunt Sue, and like her defies the whites and dies on the land, "his face buried in the wet, blurred green" (*Uncle Tom's Children,* p. 102), his body returned to the earth.

As they leave their land, Wright's characters become corrupted. Thus, in *The Long Dream* Tyree Tucker enriches himself at the expense of poor blacks. Since the tale is set in the rural South, he attempts to fulfill his familial responsibility but he lacks the Old Testament dignity which Wright's peasants exhibit. As a member of the black bourgeoisie, he has lost touch with nature and his people. Instead of tilling the land, he exploits helpless Negroes and cooperates with crooked whites to maintain his power. But the latter betray him, and in the end he dies without dignity, like most of Wright's northern protagonists. A whorehouse, not the countryside, provides the setting for Tyree's death. Tainted by his father's connections and afraid, Fishbelly joins the thousands of Negroes fleeing the South. At best he will, like Wright, find a place where he can live with dignity. But it is doubtful that he will discover a sanctuary which possesses the South's beauty. For along with the nightmare, Fish bids farewell to "grassy fields [and] spongy earth . . . , to [a shimmering] sun . . . and blue and yellow butterflies" (*The Long Dream,* p. 102). Gone is the terror but also the innocence of his youth, an innocence which Wright's urban rebels never know.

Unfortunately, in the industrialized North black peasants "encounter experiences that tend to break down the structure of [their] folk characters" (*Twelve Million Black Voices,* p. 116). "The streets, with their noises and glaring lights, the taverns, the automobiles, and the poolrooms claim them" (p. 117). "Perhaps never in history has a more unprepared folk wanted to go to the city" (p. 93), Wright observes. Unlike Bok, Wright's characters are full of illusions and are shattered to discover that non-English-speaking immigrants have more opportunity than native born Negroes.[4] The city, which destroys Wright's Negroes, allows Malamud's refugees to transplant their "lost world of . . . shtetls. . . . Malamud's distinctive settings—dark and disconsolate rooms, barred doors, groceries in cellars—are the tangible signs of [his characters'] alienation"[5] as they are in Wright's fiction, but the urban ghetto is also the scene of the victim's spiritual salvation.

Malamud's protagonists are tested by a harsh urban environment, and while some, like Wright's characters, are defeated by poverty and a fierce climate, others are redeemed by their community's concern. Thus, in "The Mourners" Kessler, an old recluse who has abandoned his family, is evicted finally from his "decrepit tenement flat" (*The Magic Barrel*, p. 17). "The rain turns to sleet [and then to] snow" (p. 22), emphasizing the old man's plight as he sits ignored on the sidewalk. But the indifference of passersby (a common occurrence in the city) is balanced by his neighbors' kindnesses. "An old Italian woman from the top floor" (p. 22) is so upset by the sight that her sons must "carry him upstairs" while another neighbor "cuts open the padlock" to his apartment. A "plate of hot macaroni" sent by the old woman also indicates that the city contains compassionate people as well as the insensitive janitor and greedy landlord who evict him. Moved by their generosity, Kessler repents and is able to arouse his landlord's sympathy. An act of "rachmones" (mercy) transforms a small, smelly room into one which is "clean, drenched in daylight and fragrance" (p. 26). Ghetto life creates many indignities, but it also encourages Malamud's characters to become involved with each other.

In the icy, snowy city both death and rebirth are possible. Thus, in "Angel Levine" a desperate tailor is saved by his new found faith in a black angel. At the story's end Manischevitz returns to his cold flat and finds that his dying wife has recovered fully. The "miracle" is accompanied by falling snow which the tailor takes for angel feathers. Similar miracles and acts of charity occur in "Idiots First," where a dying old man is permitted to save his retarded thirty-nine-year-old son. Like Kessler, Mendel encounters both cruelty and compassion on a "cold . . . bleak . . . November night" (*Idiots First*, p. 4). A pawnbroker refuses to give him enough money to send his son to a relative in California; a Jewish philanthropist contemptuously offers him food instead of train fare; but a shrunken old rabbi parts with his fur-lined caftan to help them. As Mendel rushes to the train, he is confronted by death in the guise of Ginzburg who threatens to "freeze [him] to pieces" (p. 14). A blast of "unbearable cold like an icy dagger invade[s] his body" but when death sees his own "awful wrath mirrored in Mendel's eyes" (p. 15), even he is moved to allow the father to place his son on the train.

In Malamud's works the coldest hearts can "take pity," humanity can thrive in a frigid city; and winter can turn into spring. *The Assistant* opens on a dark November morning with Morris Bober warming himself with a cup of coffee and reflecting about hard times in the city. Winter, the most common season in Malamud's fiction, approaches prematurely, and the grocer identifies his bleak existence with the blustery weather. He imagines himself unprotected, frozen on the sidewalk, a fate which he suffers at the novel's end when he collapses and dies from shovelling snow. Images abound of the grocer, his daughter Helen, and his assistant Frank Alpine, being tormented by ice and snow. The cold penetrates their dark, tomb-like store, the "drab five-room flat" (p. 19), and the grocery cellar which initially houses Frank and is symbolic of the life he has chosen. But the funereal setting and dreary weather are magically altered when Frank and Helen fall in love. They embrace in a tiny room which is filled suddenly with "flowers . . . [and the air of] a sweet spring night" (p. 138). To a great extent the environment reflects the characters' moods and behavior. Later, in the park,when Frank "rapes" Helen, a warm night turns cold, "the spring-like loveliness" (p. 165) vanishes as "they sink to their knees on the winter earth" (p. 167). Similarly, the store and the neighborhood are more depressing before Alpine arrives and after he is fired. The friendship which develops between the grocer and his assistant brightens their moods and the setting. It is almost cozy as Morris and Frank share chores and exchange confidences; their relationship offers protection against the howling wind and cheerless grocery.

In Wright's fiction a brutal city stifles compassion and breeds callousness; in Malamud's works, as mentioned in chapter 3, love transforms the environment. Frank's gentle touch turns a "wooden rose plucked from the garbage can into a real flower" (p. 245). The grave into which he falls becomes the scene of his resurrection. Objectively the grocery is a cold, depressing tomb, but it offers Alpine warmth and shelter. Reversing the American pioneering pattern, the young Italian drifts from West coast to East, and establishes his roots in an urban ghetto where he encounters all kinds of people. As a microcosm of the world, the city includes the depraved Ward Minogue, the selfish Pearls and Karps, and the compassionate grocer and his daughter.

Life is very intense in Malamud's city; a frenetic pace and overcrowding make it impossible for people to avoid each other. The potential for emotional clashes and destructive conflicts increases, but so does the opportunity to practice self-discipline and establish communities. In *The Tenants*, Malamud's most pessimistic urban novel, Harry Lesser, a hermit writer, finds it impossible to maintain his privacy. Even a condemned tenement building cannot protect against involvement with others. On a cold winter morning Harry is thrust into a relationship with a neurotic black writer, Willie Spearmint, who offers companionship, but who also threatens to disrupt his life. Through their encounter Lesser meets Irene, a Jewish girl with whom he falls in love, and blacks who resent him. Stinking halls, peeling plaster, broken windows and stairs, provide the backdrop for tragedy, but it is the protagonists' rigid personalities which make disaster inevitable. The "deadly jungle" (p. 12) is also described as a "sceptered isle on a silver sea" (p. 5) on which love briefly flowers. At one time the old building had housed families; a small roof garden with "potted flowering plants, window boxes of pansies and geraniums, and wicker chairs" (p. 11) had brought nature into the city. People had civilized the jungle, but once the stable residents had died or moved away, mold and decay set in. As Lesser's and Spearmint's relationship deteriorates, the stench increases; "huge ferns . . . and mossy trees . . . thicken and spread into the hall and down the stairs" (p. 229). Primitive bush advances and reclaims the concrete island. The city becomes uncivilized because people have abdicated their responsibilities to each other. Although *The Tenants'* setting most closely resembles the environment in Wright's works and is the bleakest of Malamud's urban landscapes, it encourages more intimacy and honesty than the rural countryside of *A New Life*.

In the latter novel a young Jewish intellectual, who attempts to escape a troubled New York past, journeys West, in a reversal of Frank Alpine's odyssey.[6] Seymour Levin seeks his promised land in Eastchester, Oregon, a small college town where mountains, not skyscrapers dominate the scenery. Levin exchanges New York pollution and dingy streets for fresh air and open spaces. He leaves behind northern winters, snow and ice and acclimates himself to the gentle Oregon rain. Both the weather and the countryside are symbolic of the local people, a bland, amiable group who are comfortable in their homogeneity. The college old-timers take pride in the community's frontier "togetherness" which emphasizes a superficial congeniality. Although initially delighted by the change in atmosphere, Levin soon feels out of place. While a rural environment fortifies Wright's characters, it isolates Malamud's. Lonely, Levin longs for substantial relationships, but his New York Jewish intensity frightens the complacent natives who fear demanding people. "Levin wanted friendship and got friendliness; he wanted steak and they offered spam" (*A New Life*, p. 125). Repeatedly he is rejected, and Pauline Gilley's description of Eastchester as a "sheltered . . . , landlocked . . . , and self-satisfied" (p. 19) community proves accurate. Unsuited to the temperate climate and lazy pace, he "arouses resentment and resistance . . . by pushing too hard" (p. 29). Misinterpreted as Eastern aggressiveness, Levin's forthrightness alienates him from most of his colleagues. Only Joseph Bucket, unable to complete his thesis on the digressive *Tristram Shandy*, sympathizes with the outcast. "Weary of making enemies, sick to death of fighting alone, living alone" (p. 319), Levin clings to Pauline, another Eastchester misfit.

Later, when the affair threatens his security, Levin considers flight but remains with Pauline. Unable and unwilling to stay in the rural Northwest, they head East. Levin's final destination is unknown, but it is quite possible that he will, like the geese he observes, return home. A year in Oregon has taught Levin that nature's "beauty is not all" (p. 366), that the quality of human nature is more important. Life in urban America may be painful, but it is also vital and alive with "the movement and mystery of people on dark . . . streets" (*A New Life*, p. 75).

Ironically, the American city, which destroys Wright's Negroes, disrupting their families and communities, sustains Malamud's Jews, enabling them to cease their wandering and establish roots. Culture, history, opportunity, and temperament give Malamud's city dwellers advantages over Wright's persecuted, semiliterate Negroes. Thus, when the two groups meet in the urban setting, the result is a clash of traditions and interests which will be examined in chapter 5.

5

A Bittersweet Encounter

It is painful when images meant to marry repel
each other
Bernard Malamud, *The Tenants*

For many years American Jews and Negroes were considered allies in the struggle against discrimination. Jewish leaders prided themselves on their contributions to civil rights while Negro spokesmen exhorted their followers to imitate Jewish unity. Differences were played down, similarities stressed. When tensions appeared, they were dismissed as exceptional. But recent events have caused both groups to question the traditional coalition. Competition for jobs, housing, and political power has increased. No longer are blacks willing to accept their status as second class citizens. They demand control over their schools, their organizations, and their communities which some believe have been influenced, if not dominated, by well-meaning Jewish liberals. In turn, Jews have been frightened by militant rhetoric, ghetto riots, and a rising black crime rate. They cannot understand why their charity has been rejected and their motives questioned. Furthermore, the identification of some black spokesmen with Arab aspirations and Third World goals worries Jewish-Americans who support Israel. Considering that Jews and Negroes have fared differently in America, the rift was perhaps inevitable.

More than twenty years ago James Baldwin analyzed Negro ambivalence towards Jews. In a perceptive essay entitled "The Harlem Ghetto," Baldwin describes the bittersweet encounter between the two minorities. On the one hand, Negroes identify with Old Testament Jews as fellow victims. "The images of the suffering Christ and the suffering Jew are wedded with the image of the suffering slave, and they are one."[1] On the other hand, Negroes inherit the prejudice of white Christians who label Jews Christ-killers. Thus, the black church spawns both sympathy and contempt for Jews. As fellow victims, Jews are expected to be more sensitive to black suffering, more compassionate and generous than other whites. When they are not, when they respond selfishly, exploiting their black customers, servants, and tenants, they are bitterly reviled. Yet, those Jews who take their liberal tradition seriously are also resented and accused of paternalism. Baldwin concludes that America has made it impossible for the two groups to trust each other and to treat each other as equals.

Since "The Harlem Ghetto" was published, black-Jewish relationships have deteriorated further. Baldwin attempted to understand Negro-Jewish interaction; compassion and sympathy for both groups dominate his essay. But the quest for black power has made some Afro-Americans outspoken and vitriolic. Angry intellectuals like Harold Cruse, Addison Gayle, Jr., and Imamu Baraka vent their frustration on Jews, accusing them of controlling the literary establishment, manipulating black culture, and undermining black independence. In turn, some Jewish writers have altered their image of Negroes. In Saul Bellow's *Henderson the Rain King* (1959), Africa is a source of life, rejuvenating the joyless, neurotic white protagonist. In *Mr. Sammler's Planet* (1970) a black pickpocket accosting Mr. Sammler, a concentration camp survivor, inspires fear. In Bruce Jay Friedman's *The Dick* (1970), Kenneth LePeters worries about his daughter's black classmates whose language and values threaten him. Similarly, Norman Podhoretz confesses his fear of Negroes in "My Negro Problem—and Ours."

But the interaction has not been completely negative. From the perspective of Richard Wright and Bernard Malamud, admiration, affection, and attraction as well as envy, hostility, and revulsion characterize black-Jewish relationships. Both authors explore and perceive the bittersweet encounter similarly. Jewish concern and charity embarrasses and sometimes humiliates black people. In *Black Boy, Native Son,* and "The Man Who Went To Chicago," Wright depicts Negro ambivalence towards Jews, who are both appreciated and resented. In all three works Jews are able to provide financial and emotional support to the underprivileged. Although well-intentioned, Jewish aid engenders envy, shame, and hostility as well as gratitude. From the Jewish perspective the encounter is also frustrating, sometimes tragic, and occasionally rewarding. Three of Malamud's works—"Angel Levine," "Black Is My Favorite Color," and *The Tenants*—emphasize the importance of mutual respect and assistance in establishing real friendships. This chapter will focus on the interaction of Negroes and Jews in Malamud's and Wright's work. But before turning to their writings, it is helpful to examine the authors' personal experiences with members of the other group.

Bernard Malamud describes in a letter his childhood impressions of Negroes who lived nearby him. The young "basketball players [appeared] vital, vigorous, skilled, a laughing kind of people [who] enjoyed their game and made me like it." Malamud also remembers "pretty black girls in brightly colored dresses."[2] At the same time he was painfully aware of Negro poverty and shame, of "women carrying heavy bundles" and others trying "to tame unruly kinky hair" (pp. 1–2). Although Malamud's parents were poor immigrants, they seemed more prosperous than their black neighbors. Consequently young Malamud who "empathized with poor people and victims of other misfortunes" wanted to share his few possessions with Buster, a black boy who had none. The "friendship" collapsed when Malamud teased him with a remark about watermelon, and Buster responded by hitting him. The incident provided the seeds for "Black Is My Favorite Color."

As an adult in the late 1930s Malamud taught English and creative writing in a Harlem evening high school. He recalls his "disappointment" in reading "soap opera" instead of "Black Literature." But he took advantage of the opportunity to survey the neighborhood, to "look into stores and watch people." One student "Alexander Levine, a black Jew" provided material for the short story "Angel Levine" and helped influence Malamud's attitude towards suffering. "I liked the concept of a Black Jew," Malamud writes in the same letter. "Perhaps it was then I thought 'All men are Jews, though they may not know it.' " The notion that all men suffer, thereby sharing a common fate, underlies Malamud's fiction, but the author rightly insists that the remark has been grossly misinterpreted by critics. He never intended to suggest that all men (Jews, blacks, and Italians among others) are identical in behavior and culture. Beyond a common vulnerability to misfortune and suffering, people have distinctive traditions, personalities, and destinies. Thus, while Malamud felt sympathy for blacks, he also "had a sense of them as people with a fate of their own." Furthermore, he admits to a "diffused, inexplicable fear of Blacks, the sort [his] mother felt about gypsies, and some gentiles felt about Jews. The fears of the other man's strangeness."

Malamud's candid letter reveals an ambivalence about black-Jewish relationships. The author is sympathetic to but also wary of the blacks he meets. Despite his lower class background, he is better off than blacks and able to help them. But his "superior" position and the differences between Negro and Jewish cultures, virtually assure his role as an outsider and an observer. Although he admires black grace and vitality (traits also lauded by Saul Bellow, and Norman Podhoretz) he never mentions respecting black intellectual achievements. Of course his impressions and reactions were shaped by contact with poor Negroes in the 1920s and 1930s. Malamud is aware, however, that Jewish charity and guidance antagonize blacks and emphasizes this in "Black Is My Favorite Color" and in *The Tenants*. The two works (more fully discussed later) illustrate the difficulty of fostering respect and friendship between individuals of disparate cultures, histories, and status.

If Malamud's superior position hindered his association with Negroes, Wright's subordinate position prevented him from feeling completely comfortable with Jews. His biography reveals his intimacy with Jews and his dependency on them. Twice he married Jewish women whose beauty, intelligence, and sensitivity appealed to him. His first marriage ended in divorce, since his wife Dhimah was too independent and unable to cater to Wright's needs. His second marriage succeeded, apparently because Ellen Poplar was devoted to her husband and offered him "stability."[3] Wright, however, was aware that her immigrant Jewish parents never accepted him and that her white skin gave her certain advantages. When the Wrights wanted to purchase a house in liberal Greenwich Village, they had to rely on their Jewish lawyer, Jacob Salzman to negotiate the deal secretly.

Professionally Wright also found himself dependent on Jewish liberals. As an impoverished young writer in Chicago, he gained employment with the help of Mary Wirth, wife of the Jewish sociologist Louis Wirth, who later "obliged him by providing a program of readings in sociology that Wright conscientiously followed."[4] The Communist party offered Wright the opportunity to meet other writers, many of whom were Jewish. At the Federal Negro

Theater Wright worked with director "Charles De Sheim, a talented Jew."[5] Jews offered money, personal and literary advice, protection against racism, and love, all of which Wright needed and appreciated. But such assistance also emphasized his helplessness and dependency.

Not surprisingly, Wright's ambivalence about Jews appears in his writing. More preoccupied with racism than Malamud is with anti-Semitism, he does not devote a complete work to minority interaction, but incorporates incidents involving blacks and Jews in the three works mentioned earlier. Despite Wright's limited treatment of Jewish-Negro relationships, it is possible to discern the pattern which Malamud develops more fully. According to *Black Boy,* black anti-Semitism originated in the church and home. Parents "generally approved" of it; the fundamentalists encouraged it. "Antagonism towards Jews," Wright observed, "was bred in [Negroes] from childhood; it was not merely racial prejudice, it was part of their cultural heritage" (*Black Boy,* p. 54). Thus, in the eyes of Wright and his young friends, Jews had committed the unpardonable sin; they had murdered the Lord. A ditty sung by young Wright and his friends echoed the sentiments of anti-Semitic white Christians;

> Bloody Christ Killers
> Never trust a Jew
> Bloody Christ Killers
> What won't a Jew do?
> (*Black Boy,* p. 71)

Like Baldwin, Wright realized that Jews occupied a precarious position in America and therefore provided safe targets for Negro frustration. "Georgia has the Negro," Baldwin had written, "and Harlem has the Jew."[6] To which Wright would have added that anti-Semitism existed wherever ignorance, poverty, and despair flourished in the North or the South. To make matters worse Jews did not appear as traditional victims. Although socially ostracized by some white Christians, they were the proprietors, the merchant class, owners of the corner grocery or black movie house. Poor blacks patronized them and often were exploited. The Southern Jew's insecurity made Wright distrust him. Thus, when he covertly tried borrowing library books, he refrained from seeking the help of Don, a

Jewish co-worker, whose "frantic desire to demonstrate a racial solidarity with whites . . . might make him betray [Wright]" (*Black Boy*, p. 215). Both Southern Negroes and Jews found it easier to turn on each other than on white Christians.

The complexity of Negro-Jewish relations increased as Wright travelled North. In the more subtly racist North blacks entered a "no man's land"[7] in human relations, never knowing precisely what to expect from whites and especially from Jews. In "The Man Who Went To Chicago," Wright explores the intricacy of ethnic interaction. Having newly arrived in the city, he applies for a job as an assistant to a Jewish delicatessen owner. Superficially the relationship with a Jewish employer reinforces Wright's Southern experience. Repelled by the Hoffmans' strange speech and mannerisms, he is aware that they are foreigners and resents the fact that they "could operate a store and earn a living in a neighborhood where [he] could not even live" (*Eight Men,* p. 212). But the Hoffmans' kindness makes it difficult for Richard to hate them. Despite his intuition, however, that the Hoffmans are decent and fair-minded, he still does not trust them. Thus, when he misses work to take a civil service exam for a postal position, he lies, afraid that revealing his ambition will cause him to lose his job. Unfortunately Wright and the Hoffmans misjudge each other. Unaware of the Negro's vulnerability and his unique psychological defenses, the kindly Jewish immigrants insist on an honest explanation from Wright. Instead of just dismissing him, laughing the matter off, or ignoring his lies, they "stood their ground and probed at [him]. It dawned on [him] that they were trying to treat [him] as an equal" (p. 217). Ironically, he finds the situation intolerable. It is one thing for whites to be economically dominant, but another for them to be morally superior. He cannot confess his dishonesty and "reveal [his] own sense of insecurity. . . . It would have been shameful . . . , [and] given them a moral advantage over [him] that would have been unbearable" (p. 217). Unable to tolerate their pity, Wright quits his job.

It is relatively easy to deal with a brutal oppressor. Hate and anger become weapons to protect oneself, violence to avenge. But how should an oppressed Negro respond to a well-meaning Jew who insists on "understanding" him? Jewish assistance, friendship, and sympathy only underscore blacks' impotency, the extent of their reliance on beneficent whites. Furthermore, white liberalism raises black expectations. Having experienced the Hoffmans' altruism, Wright is disappointed with the Jewish doctors he meets as a hospital orderly. Always curious and hungry for knowledge, he questions them about their experiments, but they ignore or mock him. Anticipating patience and sensitivity he is unprepared for the young Jewish efficiency expert who commands him to clean the seventeen rooms in "four hours and forty-nine minutes" (p. 242). Wright's bitterness is reinforced by the daily sight of "young Jewish boys and girls receiving instruction in chemistry and medicine" (p. 238), while black boys cleaned labs and "Black girls, old, fat, dressed in ragged gingham, walking loosely, carried tin cans of soap powder, rags, mops, brooms" (p. 237).

Wright's ambivalence towards Jews is developed most fully in *Native Son*. Bigger Thomas resents the Jews who own so many businesses in Chicago's Black Belt, but he values his Jewish lawyer's assistance. For the first time in his life, he meets a white who seems concerned about him. Yet the relationship also unsettles Bigger who becomes vulnerable after he learns to trust Max. Helpless, he "felt that he was sitting and holding his life . . . in his hands, waiting for Max to tell him what to do with it; and it made him hate himself" (p. 211). By breaking down Bigger's defenses, his hatred of whites, by encouraging him to analyze racism and to communicate his feelings, Max acquires tremendous power over his black client. Not only is he responsible for his defense but for his soul as well. One wrong glance or word can shatter Bigger's confidence and faith. Unfortunately Max, like the well-meaning Hoffmans, cannot truly empathize with blacks. Culturally and morally on "another planet" (p. 353), he is horrified by Bigger's rationalization of murder. Like Mrs. Dalton and white America, he is blind to the black rebel's unique sensibility. Although hurt and disappointed, Bigger does not appear surprised when his lawyer gropes "for the [cell] door, keeping his face averted" (p. 358). Instead the youth, sentenced to death, "smiles a faint, wry, bitter smile" (p. 359), acknowledging that he will die alone as he has lived.

Native Son highlights the differences between Afro-Americans and Jewish-Americans which make empathy impossible. Max views Negroes and Jews merely as victims of capitalism, but he is wrong. While he is called a "dirty Jew" (p. 295) for helping Bigger, the latter is despised solely for his color. The Jewish lawyer chooses to be a victim by embracing communism and its causes; the black rebel has no such choice. With all his education and sophistication Max is unable to appreciate emotionally what Bigger knows instinctively—that the plight of black Americans is unique, not comparable to the persecution of Communists, union activists, or Jews. While both Jews and Negroes may be hated, they are perceived differently by white Christians. Jewish craftiness and radical ideas threaten white America. Thus, Jan Erlone, a white Communist suspected of murdering Mary Dalton, is thought to be Jewish, because of his politics and association with Bigger. Automatically the police and reporters assume that trouble-making Jewish Communists have manipulated naive Negroes like Bigger who do not have the intelligence, nerve, and energy to act independently. Detective Britten goes so far as to question the Dalton housekeeper about Bigger exhibiting any Jew-like behavior, " 'waving his hands around . . . talking like Jews' " (p. 163). While Jews are viewed as cunning instigators, Negroes are considered dumb brutes. After his capture, Bigger is likened to a big black muscular ape, despite the fact that he is physically slight. By contrast, Max, the Jewish lawyer, appears verbally adept, aggressively attacking society's mores with his pointed words while Bigger looks on helplessly. The Negro is despised while the Jew is feared but also admired.

Malamud's view of Negro-Jewish relationships parallels Wright's. In two short stories and one novel, blacks appear in subordinate roles which provide a poor basis for a genuine alliance with Jews. Only "Angel Levine" comes close to realizing a balanced relationship between the two minorities. But an analysis of the tale must account for two elements which distinguish it from "Black Is My Favorite Color" and from The Tenants. Firstly, the confrontation is between a white and a black Jew who share certain cultural similarities. Secondly, the story is surrealistic, set in a twilight zone between fantasy and reality. Because Levine is both black and Jewish, a synthesis of two experiences occurs; but interestingly it is still the Jewish tradition which even in fantasy dominates and offers the possibility of salvation to both characters.

As the tale begins, Levine, a probationary angel, has appeared in the apartment of Manischevitz, a poor tailor, who has been sorely tested by God through a series of material and emotional misfortunes. Having lost his shop through fire, his son in war, his daughter to a "lout" (*The Magic Barrel*, p. 43), Manischevitz is desperate. In addition he is burdened by backaches and an ailing wife. From the outset his situation is different from that of the Hoffmans or Mr. Max. The tailor is the one in need of assistance. His concern is survival. The stage is set for the poor Jew's encounter with a Negro who can help *him*. But Malamud has not simply reversed roles, creating a black benefactor. Instead Levine's own survival is dependent on Manischevitz's acceptance. Each has what the other needs.

Before a solution is possible, however, the tailor's prejudice must be dissolved. When Levine first appears in the shabby apartment, Manischevitz is frightened and then reassures himself that the Negro is a social worker, sent to investigate his problems. In a sense Levine is a social worker but not from the Welfare Department. The angel can work miracles, alleviate pain but only if the Jew has faith. Though desperate, Manischevitz refuses to believe that a Negro can be an angel. " 'Is this what a Jewish angel looks like? . . . If God sends an angel, why a black? Why not a white that there are so many of them?' " (p. 47) Such bigotry disappoints Levine who departs for his other "home," Harlem.

In order for their relationship to develop, the Jew must admit his error, but he is not yet ready to do so. Though Manischevitz journeys to Harlem to seek Levine's help, he still views black life critically. Harlem is frightening, a "dark world. It was vast and its light lit nothing. Everywhere were shadows, often moving" (p. 49). "Fear of the other man's strangeness"[8] makes the tailor view Negroes as shadows, much as they view themselves in Wright's works. An outsider in Harlem, Manischevitz forces himself to enter Bella's black cabaret, the nether world of Negro life to which Levine has descended. There, in the noisy, vulgar, debilitating atmosphere, he finds a changed Levine. The shabby suit, the sad but dignified expression have been exchanged for a "drunken look . . . and a shiny new checkered suit, pearl gray derby, cigar, and big two-toned button shoes" (p. 54). The Negro's formerly mournful Jewish appearance has been replaced by black ostentation; his Jewish spirituality converted into black sensualism as he fondles the uncouth Bella. Levine's metamorphosis from God's messenger to Satan's playmate seems complete. Only the poor tailor's faith can reverse the process. Despite his fears, despite the black patrons' taunts, Manischevitz approaches Levine, who eyes him suspiciously. The Jew must come to the Negro, seek his assistance, on his terms, in his environment. Once he finally professes faith, the miracle can occur. Shedding the Harlem identity, Levine changes into his old clothes; and Manischevitz returns home to find his wife recovered and cleaning the apartment. A flutter of "magnificent black wings" and a falling white feather indicate that Levine too has been rewarded, accepted into heaven.

The story ends on a positive note with both characters prospering. But unfortunately this is a poor prescription for black-Jewish relations. The Negro is accepted only when he sheds his black identity and assumes a Jewish one. Jewishness dominates, submerging blackness. There appears to be no room in heaven for *black* angels as evidenced by Manischevitz's assumption that the heavenly feather, like the Heavenly Father, is white. Whiteness is associated with saintliness, blackness with decadence. Positive black values are missing from this story, which imposes Jewish tradition on Negroes. In a synagogue four black Jews discuss " 'neshoma' " (soul) and conclude that skin color is immaterial, that all men have soul, a rosy deduction absent from Malamud's later fiction. But is the elimination of color distinction worthwhile if it requires that blacks become Jewish? Implicit is the assumption of Jewish moral superiority, which hardly would have been acceptable to Richard Wright and is even less so to contemporary black militants.

Malamud appears to have recognized this in "Black Is My Favorite Color" and *The Tenants,* which examine black resentment toward Jewish superiority. The short story is told from the perspective of Nat Lime, a Jewish storekeeper who cannot understand why Negroes spurn his friendship. He recalls his childhood spent in a poor white neighborhood which contained a "block of run-down dirtier [Negro] frame houses" (*Idiots First,* p. 19). At the edge of poverty himself, Nat nevertheless "was old enough to know [that he] was better off" (p. 20) than Buster Wilson, the black youth with a drunken, brutal father. Loneliness, perhaps Buster's independence, attracted Nat to him. Though repelled and frightened by black life, by the drunken brawls, the gambling, and obscenities, he is also drawn (as Malamud was) to the music, the laughter, the colorfully dressed girls. He spends as much time as he can in the black community and attempts to befriend Buster. But the association is doomed from the start, for young Nat does not realize that friendship cannot be bought, that the "gifts" he urges on Buster humiliate the black boy and cause him to reject the Jewish youth. Tired of being given things, of being exposed to Nat's critical eyes which register pity and dismay at black poverty and brutality, Buster rebels, venting his humiliation in a violent attack on the Jewish boy. " 'Jew bastard,' " he exclaims. " 'Take your Jew movies and your Jew candy and shove them up your Jew ass' " (p. 22). To preserve his self-respect Buster must reject Nat's charity.

Though Nat vaguely realizes later that "you can't force it" (p. 23), he still continues to seek relationships with blacks. He is compelled to be his brother's keeper, and thus reaps the consequences. The mere act of picking up a black woman's glove results in rejection. " 'I don't like white men trying to do me favors' " (p. 23), he is told. Later when the same woman, Mrs. Ornita Harris, appears in his Harlem liquor shop, Nat instinctively offers her a discount. Though attracted to Ornita, he cannot help evaluating her, noting that "her face was pretty, with big eyes and high cheek bones, but lips a little thick and nose a little broad" (p. 24). In that "but" reside his reservations about negritude. Despite protests to the contrary, Lime cannot forget that both Ornita and Buster are Negroes, different than himself.

On his first awkward date with Ornita, he reflects that they behaved as strangers who "were chained" (p. 24) together. The image could serve as a metaphor for Negro-Jewish relations. Nat is estranged from the blacks he meets, but there is also a bond. The struggle continues. The Jew makes overtures; the black resists. Nat's affair with Ornita is counterpointed by his being beaten and robbed by two black men. The night Ornita returns his love, Nat is again attacked by blacks, this time for trespassing on "Black pussy" (p. 29). Despite assertions that he's no "Jew landlord" (p. 28) but a generous merchant who pays his colored clerks well, Nat again becomes the victim of black wrath. For he has committed the unforgivable: he has threatened the masculinity of insecure Negroes. The end is predictable; Ornita is forced to reject Nat, who can only complicate her life. The well-meaning Malamudian Jew almost begs for victimization through his inability to understand the Negro's emotional conflicts and his incapacity to learn from past experiences.

The story ends as it has begun: Nat persists in trying to get his cleaning woman, ironically named Charity Sweetness, to stop eating in the bathroom and instead join him at the table. As he lavished gifts on Buster, love on Ornita, so he imposes his notion of equality on an old black cleaning woman trained by white society not to take her place at the table. No wonder Nat's overtures are rejected. Nevertheless the consequences are tragic. Ornita, ready for love, Buster for friendship, must deny their needs. Nat's desire to give is also thwarted. Worse, he does not perceive his own role in the frustrating relationships. By narrating the tale from Nat's viewpoint, Malamud allows the reader to sympathize with him but also to see through his self-pity and rationalizations of failure. "The drama," writes Sidney Richman, "is compounded by the nature of the subject ['a victim amid victims'] and particularly by Nat's lack of insight into a story more ambiguous and more agonized than most."[9]

Richman's remarks also apply to *The Tenants,* which reveals Malamud's growing pessimism about black-Jewish relations. Society itself has changed since the late fifties when Malamud penned "Angel Levine." No longer are blacks interested in acceptance at the expense of their identity. Tension, conflict, and angry rhetoric have taken over as Jews and Negroes battle each other in the struggle to survive in the urban jungle. *The Tenants* is faithful to these contemporary events. Set in New York City, it explores the interaction of Harry Lesser and Willie Spearmint, a Jewish and a black writer. The encounter embraces more than two individuals. It is a clash of two traditions: the intellectual and the sensual; a debate between two aesthetics: the rational and the radical. The protagonists enact roles assigned them by centuries of conditioning.

The cerebral, self-disciplined, passive Lesser is the quintessential Jewish victim, suffering and sacrificing for art, his religion. For Lesser the word is deed; intellect has replaced action; love is analyzed not experienced. By contrast, the passionate, irrational, spirited Spearmint is the black rebel, acting impulsively, demanding immediate gratification. Although both are writers, their literary attitudes, abilities, and experiences are strikingly different. The Jew writes about love, emphasizing universal themes. The black spews hatred, violence, stressing a particular rage. Fearing artistic chaos and disintegration, Lesser preaches the importance of "form" (*The Tenants,* p. 75) and discipline, which Spearmint rejects in favor of raw emotion. " 'Art can kiss my juicy ass, ' " he proclaims. " 'I am art. Willie Spearmint, *Black man.* My form is myself' " (p. 75). When the outraged Spearmint heaps obscenities on the Jews, Lesser politely describes his opponent's " 'mouth as a place of excrement' " (p. 132). In addition to their aesthetic and stylistic differences, both have different literary objectives. Lesser seeks love and meaning through writing while Spearmint desires wealth and status.

Given these differences, a tragic conflict appears inevitable in the condemned tenement which both occupy. Moreover, their cultural discord is exacerbated by the sexual competition described in chapter 3. All that prevents the two from immediately destroying each other is the recognition that they also need each other. A published author with a little money, Lesser can offer advice, guidance, and shelter to the untutored and impoverished black. In turn, Spearmint introduces the Jew to sex and then to love, allowing him temporarily to blossom as a man and revitalize his writing. Both represent extreme personalities and can benefit by adopting some of the other's traits. Unfortunately the friendship is never realized. The cultural differences between black and Jew are much greater than those between Italian and Jew in *The Assistant,* for example. Furthermore, Spearmint is not like Alpine or Angel Levine, who willingly embrace Judaic tradition. From the moment he leaves his typewriter and then his manuscript in Lesser's care, he resents him. Dependency breeds self-hatred, exasperation, and ultimately violence as Spearmint realizes that the economically and professionally superior Jew is influencing his personality and literary style. The relationship remains unbalanced for, like Nat Lime, Lesser has the advantage over blacks. As Cynthia Ozick has observed, "Lesser is always the pro, the polished authority, patron of opinion; he has published before. . . . Willie, out of the ghetto, is the rough hewn disciple."[10] Supported by a long literary and intellectual tradition, the Jew has mastered techniques of form and style and needs only to immerse himself in experience to resuscitate his writing. Spearmint's task is more difficult. Though powerful, his work lacks cohesiveness. His background has equipped him to write energetically but not coherently. When he applies Lesser's standards, his writing deteriorates. The words seem derivative, the style artificial and stilted. Moreover, his personality is transformed. He changes from a passionate, sensual being into a nervous, frustrated writer who begins to look and sound like the Jew.

The Jew's compassion only worsens the situation. "Lack of sympathy," Cynthia Ozick has observed, "is an obvious offense;

sympathy turns out to be more offensive yet."[11] When Lesser tries to empathize, Spearmint explodes. Like Buster, Ornita, and Charity Sweetness in "Black Is My Favorite Color"; like Richard Wright, Harold Cruse and Imamu Baraka, Willie rejects Jewish benevolence and tries to assert his identity. He changes his name to Bill Spear in a pathetic attempt to assume a new, more militant, and dignified self. His writing grows angrier and more anti-Semitic. He seeks revenge for the loss of his girlfriend and his spontaneity by destroying Lesser's manuscript. When the Jew, goaded to retaliate, destroys Spearmint's typewriter, physical violence erupts. In a highly surrealistic scene Jew and black drive each other to the ultimate encounter as Lesser crushes the black man's brains, while Spearmint slashes the Jew's testicles. Lesser no longer need fear Spearmint as an artistic or intellectual threat; the destruction of his manuscript is also avenged. Spearmint, meanwhile, castrates the Jew who has stolen his girlfriend, destroyed his typewriter and his creativity. But, by destroying that which most threatens them, they also destroy themselves and the possibility of harmony between disparate peoples and cultures.

Is there no solution then? Has Malamud succumbed to pessimism as many black writers have done? Earlier in the novel Lesser dreams of wedding the two cultures. On a remote African Isle two marriages take place: Harry Lesser and Mary Kettlesmith (Spearmint's black friend) are united by an old African tribal chief who tells the Jew that words are useless, self-analysis destructive, and only enjoyment of life worthwhile. In the same dream Willie Spearmint and Irene Belinsky (the neurotic Jewish girl) are married by a traditional rabbi who stresses " 'mutual trust, insight into each other, generosity . . . , character [and sacrifice]' " (p. 216). Unfortunately Lesser and Spearmint are products of incompatible traditions and cannot accept the advice given them. The rabbi can pray that " 'God will bring together Ishmael and Israel to live as one people' " (p. 216), but the vision, Malamud realizes, is Jewish. The union of Negro and Jew under a God "the color of light" (p. 216) is offensive to blacks. It is the Jewish liberal's appeal for universal brotherhood at the expense of black independence and pride. It is the dream of Manischevitz, Nat Lime, and Harry Lesser, a "miracle" rejected by Bigger Thomas and Cross Damon.

Conditioned by disparate cultural, historical, and religious experiences, Malamud's and Wright's protagonists respond differently to alienation, persecution, and suffering. Separated from his ancestral home, enslaved physically and spiritually, the black rebel forsakes passive suffering and asserts himself violently. Sustained by ancient traditions and values, by the promise of American freedom, the Jewish victim accepts his burdens and elevates pain to a moral virtue. But if their reactions differ, their desires do not. In an increasingly mechanized and materialistic society, both rebels and victims reject conformity, celebrate freedom, and seek to affirm the worth of the individual.

NOTES

INTRODUCTION

1. Richard Wright, *The Outsider*, p. 90. Subsequent references to primary sources are given in the text, and refer to the editions listed in the bibliography.
2. Ihab Hassan, *Radical Innocence: The Contemporary American Novel*, Ch. 1 and 2.
3. Leslie Fiedler, *No! In Thunder*, p. 236.
4. James Baldwin and Ralph Ellison among others have criticized Wright for his portrayal of the black man.
5. Saunders Redding, "The Alien Land of Richard Wright," in *Reflections on Richard Wright: A Symposium on an Exiled Native Son*, ed. Donald B. Gibson, p. 64.
6. Dan McCall, *The Example of Richard Wright*, p. 193.
7. Alfred Kazin, "The Jew as Modern American Writer," in *The Commentary Reader* (Atheneum, 1966), p. xviii.
8. Ben Siegel quoted in Irving Malin, *Jews and Americans*, p. 171.
9. The black rebel appears in the works of James Baldwin, Ralph Ellison, John A. Williams while the Jewish victim is depicted by Saul Bellow, Philip Roth, Edward Lewis Wallant, and Bruce Jay Friedman.
10. Fiedler, p. 238.
11. Malin, p. 171.
12. Cross Damon in *The Outsider* appears to be Wright's only protagonist capable of analyzing and articulating his frustration.
13. Norman Mailer quoted in Allen Guttmann, *The Jewish Writer in America— Assimilation and the Crisis of Identity*, p. 162.
14. Redding, p. 65.
15. Sidney Richman, *Bernard Malamud*, p. 20.
16. "Nonethnic" refers to works where the protagonists are neither black nor Jewish. Wright's "nonethnic" novel is *Savage Holiday;* Malamud's is *The Natural.*

1: REBELS AND VICTIMS

1. Irving Malin, *Bernard Malamud and the Critics;* Leslie and Joyce Field, eds., *Jews and Americans;* and Sanford Pinsker, *The Schlemiel as Metaphor* stress the

humanism of contemporary Jewish-American literature. Addison Gayle, Jr., ed., *The Black Aesthetic* and LeRoi Jones and Larry Neal, eds., *Black Fire* emphasize the anger of contemporary black-American writing.

2. *No! In Thunder,* p. 236.
3. James A. Emanuel and Theodore L. Gross, eds., *Dark Symphony: Negro Literature in America,* p. 3.
4. Ben Siegel, "Victims in Motion: The Sad and Bitter Clowns," in Field and Field, eds., p. 123.
5. Dan McCall, *The Example of Richard Wright,* p. 123.
6. Michel Fabre, *The Unfinished Quest of Richard Wright,* p. 160.
7. *The Negro Novel in America,* p. 147.
8. *Black Skins, White Masks,* p. 122.
9. Constance Webb, *Richard Wright: A Biography,* p. 310.
10. Fabre, p. 78.
11. David Bakish, *Richard Wright,* p. 65.
12. Pinsker, p. 9.
13. "Schnorrer" is Yiddish for bothersome beggar.
14. *Radical Innocence: The Contemporary American Novel,* p. 75.
15. Sidney Richman, *Bernard Malamud,* p. 55.
16. McCall, p. 100.

2: GENESIS

1. Benjamin E. Mays, *The Image of God in Negro Literature,* pp. 66–7.
2. Mays, pp. 219–20.
3. Bernard Sherman, *The Invention of the Jew—Jewish-American Education Novels (1916-1964),* p. 62.
4. Richler's St. Urbain St. setting in *The Apprenticeship of Duddy Kravitz* and *St. Urbain's Horsemen* can be compared with Saul Bellow's and Bernard Malamud's settings.
5. "Defender of the Faith," a short story by Philip Roth, appears in *Goodbye Columbus.*
6. "Wisdom of Our Forefathers" is a collection of ethical maxims from the Talmud.
7. Margaret Walker Alexander, "Richard Wright," in David Ray and Robert Farnsworth, eds., *Richard Wright: Impressions and Perspectives,* p. 65.
8. Addison Gayle Jr. and Irving Howe are representative of the many critics who label Wright the father of militant Afro-American literature.
9. Sheldon Norman Grebstein, "Bernard Malamud and the Jewish Movement," in Irving Malin, ed., *Contemporary American-Jewish Literature,* p. 178.
10. "The Jewish Literary Tradition," in Leslie and Joyce Field, eds., *Bernard Malamud and the Critics,* p. 5.
11. Irving Howe and Eliezer Greenberg, eds., *A Treasury of Yiddish Stories,* p. 11.
12. Howe and Greenberg, p. 4.
13. Howe and Greenberg, p. 10.
14. Elizabeth Herzog and Mark Zborowski, *Life Is with People: The Jewish Little Town of Eastern Europe,* p. 216.
15. Considering Susskind's nature and his effect on Fidelman, the greeting "Shalom" (peace) is ironic.
16. Charles Alva Hoyt, "The New Romanticism," in Field and Field, eds., p. 177.
17. Sidney Richman, *Bernard Malamud,* p. 117.
18. Robert Weisbord and Arthur Stein, *Bittersweet Encounter: The Afro-American and the American Jew,* pp. 36–7.

19. The name Levitansky is derived from Levites, Jews consecrated to serve in the Tabernacle. Hence the character's Jewish mission is emphasized.
20. *Black Religion: The Negro and Christianity in the United States,* p. 35.
21. Herzog and Zborowski, p. 105.
22. Herzog and Zborowski, p. 211.
23. Herzog and Zborowski, p. 265.
24. Herzog and Zborowski, p. 112.

3: FATHERS, SONS, AND LOVERS

1. Bernard Malamud, personal communication to Evelyn Avery.
2. *Life Is with People: The Jewish Little Town of Eastern Europe,* p. 291.
3. *Life Is with People,* p. 292.
4. Irving Malin, *Jews and Americans,* p. 54.
5. Nella Larsen, *Quicksand;* Zora Neale Houston, *Jonah's Gourd Vine;* and Alice Walker, *The Third Life of Grange Copeland* typify black novels in which women are socially superior to their men.
6. Michel Fabre, *The Unfinished Quest of Richard Wright,* p. 198.
7. Carl Russell Brignano, *Richard Wright: An Introduction to the Man and his Works,* p. 18.
8. Fabre, p. 12.
9. Fabre, p. 13.
10. Herzog and Zborowski, p. 271.
11. According to Alpine, St. Francis was so lonely that he created a wife and several children "out of snow" (*The Assistant,* p. 95).
12. Bernard Sherman, *The Invention of the Jew, Jewish-American Education Novel (1916-1964),* p. 166.
13. Christof Wegelin, "The American Schlemiel Abroad; Malamud's Italian Stories and the End of American Innocence," *Twentieth Century Literature* 19 (April 1973): 81.

4: THE PROMISED LAND

1. Ralph Ellison, *Shadow and Act,* p. 136.
2. At the conclusion of *Black Boy* Wright confesses that he will never be able to forget the South which has molded his personality.
3. Michel Fabre, *The Unfinished Quest of Richard Wright,* p. 475.
4. In *Native Son* Bigger Thomas resents the Jews who own shops in black neighborhoods.
5. Sidney Richman, *Bernard Malamud,* p. 25.
6. Sanford Pinsker, *The Schlemiel As Metaphor,* p. 109.

5: A BITTERSWEET ENCOUNTER

1. James Baldwin, *Notes of a Native Son,* p. 67.
2. Bernard Malamud, personal communication to Evelyn Avery. The biographical information in this and the following paragraph came from this letter.
3. Michel Fabre, *The Unfinished Quest of Richard Wright,* p. 275.
4. Fabre, p. 232.
5. Richard Wright, *The God That Failed,* ed. Richard Cressman (1944; reprint ed., New York: Harper & Row, 1963), p. 150.
6. *Notes of a Native Son,* p. 72.

7. Robert Weisbord and Arthur Stein, *Bittersweet Encounter: The Afro-American and the American Jew*, p. 38.
8. Bernard Malamud, personal communication to Evelyn Avery, p. 2.
9. *Bernard Malamud*, p. 139.
10. Cynthia Ozick, "Literary Blacks and Jews," *Midstream* 18 (June-July 1972): 18.
11. Ozick, p. 13.

BIBLIOGRAPHY

PRIMARY SOURCES

Note: In-text references to primary sources refer to the editions listed here.

Works by Bernard Malamud:

The Assistant. New York: Farrar, Straus and Giroux, 1957.
The Magic Barrel. New York: Farrar, Straus and Giroux, 1958.
A New Life. New York: Farrar, Straus and Giroux, 1961.
Idiots First. New York: Farrar, Straus and Giroux, 1963.
The Fixer. New York: Farrar, Straus and Giroux, 1966.
Pictures of Fidelman. New York: Farrar, Straus and Giroux, 1969.
The Tenants. New York: Farrar, Straus and Giroux, 1971.
Rembrandt's Hat. New York: Farrar, Straus and Giroux, 1973.
Personal communication to Evelyn Avery. Bennington, Vermont, July 8, 1973.

Works by Richard Wright:

Uncle Tom's Children. New York: Harper and Brothers, 1940.
Native Son. New York: Harper and Brothers, 1940.
Twelve Million Black Voices: A Folk History of the Negro in the United States. New York: The Viking Press, 1941.
Black Boy: A Record of Childhood. New York: Harper and Brothers, 1945.
The Outsider. New York: Harper and Brothers, 1953.
Black Power: A Record of Reactions in a Land of Pathos. New York: Harper and Brothers, 1954.
The Long Dream. New York: Doubleday, 1958.
Eight Men. New York: World Publishing Company, 1961.
Lawd Today. New York: Walker and Company, 1963.

SECONDARY SOURCES

Bakish, David. *Richard Wright.* New York: Frederick Unger, 1973.
Baldwin, James. *Notes of a Native Son.* Boston: Beacon Press, 1955.
Bone, Robert. *The Negro Novel in America.* New Haven: Yale University Press, 1958.

Brignano, Carl Russell. *Richard Wright: An Introduction to the Man and his Works.* Pittsburgh: University of Pittsburgh Press, 1970.

Bryer, Jackson. "Richard Wright: A Selected Checklist of Criticism." *Wisconsin Studies in Contemporary Literature* 1 (Fall 1960): 22-3.

Cruse, Harold. *The Crisis of the Negro Intellectual.* New York: William Morrow & Co., 1967.

Davis, Arthur P. "*The Outsider* as a Novel of Race." *Midwest Journal* 7 (1955–56): 320–6.

Ellison, Ralph. *Shadow and Act.* New York: Random House, 1964.

Emanuel, James and Gross, Theodore L., eds. *Dark Symphony: Negro Literature in America.* New York: Free Press, 1968.

Fabre, Michel. *The Unfinished Quest of Richard Wright.* New York: William Morrow & Co., 1973.

Fanon, Frantz. *Black Skins, White Masks.* New York: Evergreen Cat Book, 1967.

Fiedler, Leslie. *No! In Thunder.* Boston: Beacon Press, 1960.

Field, Leslie A., and Field, Joyce W., eds. *Bernard Malamud and the Critics.* New York: New York University Press, 1970.

Frazier, E. Franklin. *The Negro Family in the United States.* Chicago: The University of Chicago Press, 1939.

Gayle, Addison, Jr., ed. *The Black Aesthetic.* New York: Doubleday, 1971.

– – –. *The Way of the New World: The Black Novel in America.* New York: Doubleday, 1975.

Glicksberg, Charles I. "Existentialism in *The Outsider.*" *Four Quarters* 7 (January, 1958): 17–26.

Grebstein, Sheldon Norman. "Bernard Malamud and the Jewish Movement." In *Contemporary American-Jewish Literature,* edited by Irving Malin, pp. 175–212. Bloomington: Indiana University Press, 1973.

Guttmann, Allen. *The Jewish Writer in America–Assimilation and the Crisis of Identity.* New York: Oxford University Press, 1971.

Hassan, Ihab. *Radical Innocence: The Contemporary American Novel.* Princeton: Princeton University Press, 1961.

Herzog, Elizabeth and Zborowski, Mark. *Life Is with People: The Jewish Little Town of Eastern Europe.* New York: International University Press, 1952.

Hoffman, Frederick J. *The Modern Novel in America.* Chicago: Henry Regnery, 1956.

Howe, Irving and Greenberg, Eliezer, eds. *A Treasury of Yiddish Stories.* New York: Viking Press, 1954.

Jones, LeRoi and Neal, Larry. *Black Fire: An Anthology of Afro-American Writing.* New York: William Morrow & Co., 1968.

Kazin, Alfred. "The Jew as Modern Writer." *Commentary* 41 (April 1966): 37–41.

Kosofsky, Rita N. *Bernard Malamud–An Annotated Checklist.* Kent, Ohio: Kent State University Press, 1969.

McCall, Dan. *The Example of Richard Wright.* New York: Harcourt, Brace & World, 1969.

Malin, Irving. *Jews and Americans.* Carbondale: Southern Illinois University Press, 1965.

Mandel, Ruth B. "Bernard Malamud's *The Assistant* and *A New Life:* Ironic Affirmation." *Critique* 7 (winter 1964–65): 110–21.

Mays, Benjamin E. *The Image of God in Negro Literature.* New York: Russell and Russell, 1938.

Mellard, James M. "Malamud's *The Assistant:* The City Novel in Pastoral." *Studies in Short Fiction* 5 (fall 1967): 1–11.

Ozick, Cynthia. "Literary Blacks and Jews." *Midstream* 18 (June–July 1972): 10–24.

Pinsker, Sanford. "The Achievement of Bernard Malamud." *Midwest Quarterly* 10 (summer 1969): 379–89.
———. *The Schlemiel as Metaphor.* Carbondale: Southern Illinois University Press, 1971.
Ray, David and Farnsworth, Robert. *Richard Wright: Impressions and Perspectives.* Ann Arbor: University of Michigan Press, 1973.
Redding, Saunders. "The Alien Land of Richard Wright." In *Reflections on Richard Wright: A Symposium on an Exiled Native Son,* edited by Donald B. Gibson. New York: New York University Press, 1970.
Richman, Sidney. *Bernard Malamud.* New York: Twayne Publishers, 1966.
Roth, Philip. "The New Jewish Stereotypes." *American Judaism* 11 (winter 1961): 49–51.
Rovit, Earl H. "Bernard Malamud and the Jewish Literary Tradition." *Critique* 3 (winter–spring 1960): 3–10.
Scott, Nathan A., Jr. "Search for Beliefs: The Fiction of Richard Wright." *University of Kansas City Review* 23 (1956): 19–24.
Shear, Walter. "Culture Conflict in *The Assistant.*" *Midwest Quarterly* 7 (summer 1966): 367–80.
Sherman, Bernard. *The Invention of The Jew—Jewish-American Education Novels (1916-1964).* New York: Thomas Yoseloff, 1969.
Washington, Joseph. *Black Religion: The Negro and Christianity in the United States.* Boston: Beacon Press, 1966.
Webb, Constance. *Richard Wright: A Biography.* New York: G. P. Putnam's Sons, 1968.
Wegelin, Christof. "The American Schlemiel Abroad: Malamud's Italian Stories and the End of American Innocence." *Twentieth Century Literature* 19 (April 1973): 77–88.
Weisbord, Robert and Stein, Arthur. *Bittersweet Encounter: The Afro-American and the American Jew.* Westport, Connecticut: Negro Universities Press, 1970.
Widmer, Kingsley. "The Existential Darkness: Richard Wright's *The Outsider.*" *Wisconsin Studies in Contemporary Literature* 1 (fall 1960): 13–21.

INDEX